7th Biennial Workshop on Digital Signal Processing for In-Vehicle Systems and Safety 2015

Berkeley, California, USA
14-16 October 2015

ISBN: 978-1-5108-2784-4

Printed from e-media with permission by:

Curran Associates, Inc.
57 Morehouse Lane
Red Hook, NY 12571

Some format issues inherent in the e-media version may also appear in this print version.

Printed by Curran Associates, Inc. (2016)

For permission requests, please contact University of Texas at Dallas
at the address below.

University of Texas at Dallas
800 W. Campbell Road
Richardson, Texas 75080-3021
USA

Phone: 972 883-2111

www.utdallas.edu

Additional copies of this publication are available from:

Curran Associates, Inc.
57 Morehouse Lane
Red Hook, NY 12571 USA
Phone: 845-758-0400
Fax: 845-758-2633
Email: curran@proceedings.com
Web: www.proceedings.com

TABLE OF CONTENTS

Driver prediction to improve interaction with in-vehicle HMI

Bret Harsham[1], Shinji Watanabe[1], Alan Esenther[2,5], John Hershey[1], Jonathan Le Roux[1], Yi Luan[3,5], Daniel Nikovski[1], Vamsi Potluru[4,5]

[1]: MERL, USA
E-mail: {harsham,watanabe,hershey,leroux,nikovski}@merl.com
[2]: The MathWorks, USA
E-mail: alan.esenther@mathworks.com
[3]: University of Washington, USA
E-mail: luanyi@u.washington.edu
[4]: Comcast Labs, USA
E-mail: vamsi_potluru@cable.comcast.com
[5]: *Alan Esenther, Yi Luan, and Vamsi Potluru contributed to this work while at MERL.*

Abstract Recently there has been a trend toward increasing the capability of the in-vehicle interface in terms of access to information and complex controls. This has been accompanied by an increase in the complexity of the car Human Machine Interface [HMI]. At the same time, studies have shown that driver distraction can contribute to accidents. This paper provides some possible ways to reduce driver cognitive load by augmenting the interface. We use prediction of the driver's next action or intention in order to provide UI affordances for more quickly selecting actions. Two examples of this are presented: prediction of driver interaction with the car HMI based on the driving history, and prediction of driver intention from the driver speech. In the first example, we used signal processing techniques to extract meaningful features from vehicle CAN and history data, and then we used machine learning techniques to predict the driver's next action. In the second example, we used ASR and natural language processing to extract text features from driver speech, and predict user intention using a neural network and word embedding. The proposed prediction methods for user actions and intentions can be used to improve in-vehicle task performance.

Keywords Car HMI, Prediction of driver interaction, Prediction of driver intention, Machine learning, Spoken language understanding

1. INTRODUCTION

It has been shown in numerous studies that driver distraction is linked with higher accident risk [1]. Driver distraction during performance of a secondary task is a problem that occurs both with handheld devices [2] and built-in car HMI devices [3]. While it can be difficult to predict which cognitive resources will be most likely to be overloaded by a particular task, the National Highway Traffic Safety Administration [NHTSA] has published guidelines for limiting driver distraction during interaction with a car HMI [4]. These include limiting task completion time, and limiting the amount of visual information presented to a driver during task performance. One way of achieving both of these improvements is to reduce the number of actions that a driver needs to perform and/or the number of choices offered to a driver (either visually or aurally) while performing a task. This paper looks at two separate methods for achieving this, both based on using machine learning techniques to make predictions about what the driver will do next. Based on the predictions, the user interface can be modified so that the average number of actions needed to perform a task can be reduced. This will in general reduce the task performance time.

Section 2 introduces a method for prediction of driver interaction with the car HMI based on the driving history. Modern vehicles are equipped with many different kinds of sensors which are capable of providing information about the state of the vehicle, the road network, and the occupants of the vehicle. Traffic patterns and human behavioral patterns are strongly dependent on time and circumstances. We developed a feature set based on the driving history, and unsupervised method of feature selection by ordering the feature set based on which features were most informative.

Section 3 focuses on spoken language understanding (SLU) for in-vehicle dialog systems, which predict user intentions from the output of an automatic speech recognizer (ASR) [5, 6]. In this paper we focus on two key tasks in targeted dialog and understanding applications: user intention understanding and user goal estimation. User intention understanding is the extraction of the intended meaning (called "intention" hereafter) of one user utterance, performed by the SLU module. User goal estimation is a similar concept, but is an estimation of the final system action (called "goal" hereafter) that the user wishes to accomplish during the dialog. A dialog usually consists of a series of user utterances and system actions, so the goal estimation takes place over a longer time scale than user intention understanding. Intention understanding and goal estimation are performed by employing a (recurrent) neural network with word embedding based feature augmentation and/or network pre-training [7, 8, 9, 10].

2. PREDICTION OF DRIVER INTERACTION WITH THE CAR HMI BASED ON THE DRIVING HISTORY

2.1. Data Collection

The data set used for this work was collected in Japan in several vehicles equipped with a logging system which captured driving state data from the CAN bus, and HMI event and state data from a modified car navigation system. CAN bus data is high frequency, but low level, information about the state of the car including vehicle speed, position of brake and accelerator pedal, window, shift lever, lighting and gasoline states, etc. The car nav system reported information about the current destination (such as distance, location, genre and category), map data about the road network (distance from home, distance from destination, road type, data about points of interest and roads near the vehicle, etc.), and information about the HMI state and user actions. Each of the instrumented vehicles was driven by one user at a time for a period ranging from a few days to a month, but typically approximately two weeks. Users were asked to use the car to perform scripted scenarios, such as going to a particular kind of store during a set time of the day. The scripted tasks were designed to include regular trips such as going to/from work, and also more spontaneous trips such as shopping or going to a restaurant. This is a scripted data collection, but because the users interacted with the car HMI while driving, it also contains naturalistic user actions, e.g. re-routing or changing the map view in response to driving conditions. The full data set consists of data from 26 users across 186 driving days. Our data processing and analysis treats all actions the same - we made no attempt to separate scripted actions and naturalistic actions.

2.2. Feature Processing

Many machine learning algorithms work best with indicator variables that indicate the presence or absence of a particular condition, for example, "it is rush hour". However, using hard range boundaries to determine indicator values is problematic with many of the kinds of data variables present in the data set, and with driving data in general, in the sense that users tend to take similar actions during a time range rather than always at the same time. For instance, even if morning rush hour is typically 7 am - 9 am in a particular area, if it is 9:30 in the morning, there may still be rush hour traffic, and the user may still be doing his or her typical morning actions.

Because of this, we use sampling functions to generate a set of probabilistic ("soft") indicator variables from a single data variable over a continuous range: we overlay a series of N evenly spaced Gaussian random variables G_1 - G_N on the range of the input variable. Given a particular input value x, we use the value of the probability density function $f_{G_i}(x)$ of each Gaussian at x as a sampling function, with the values normalized so that they sum to 1. This gives us a group of N soft bin indicator values I_1 - I_N representing the input value x.

$$I_m = \frac{f_{G_m}(x)}{\sum_{i\in\{1..N\}} f_{G_i}(x)} \quad (1)$$

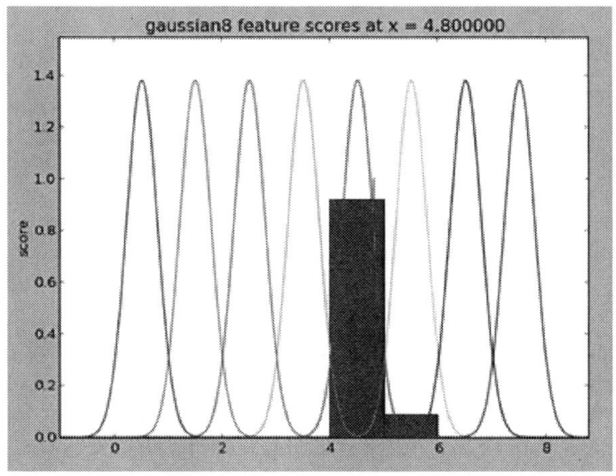

Fig. 1. *Soft bin Indicators, evenly spaced*

Figure 1 shows an example group of 8 soft indicator bins. The indicator variables change smoothly as the input value x varies over its range. This type of indicator is suitable for many kinds of data, including time data. For other kinds of data, such as the vehicle speed, it can be more suitable to use logarithmically spaced bins, as shown in Figure 2.

2.3. Prediction Models and Feature Selection

We used the Scikit-learn [11] machine learning Python framework to build several kinds of prediction models based on our features. In order to decide which features to include, we implemented an automatic method of feature selection based on repeatedly evaluating prediction performance with different sets of features groups. In general, the feature selection method is as follows:

By repeatedly removing the feature group that reduces performance the least, we first remove features that are not actually informative, thus reducing overtraining, and improving performance. As we continue to remove features, we remove the least helpful features first, generating an ordered list of how informative the features are. Figure 3 shows an example of prediction accuracy during feature selection. In this

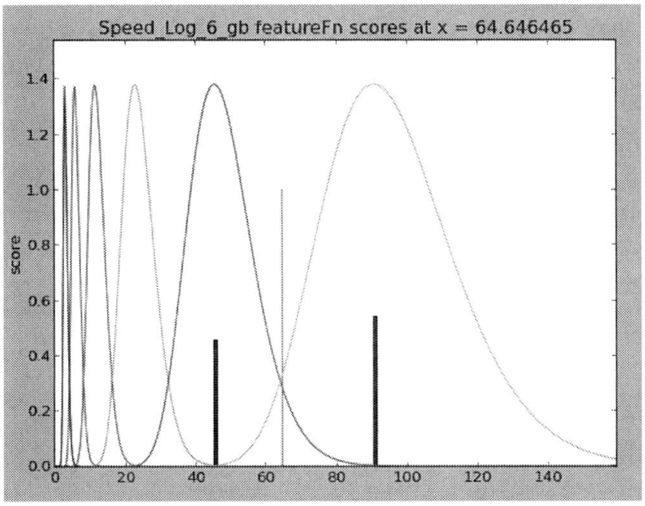

Fig. 2. *Soft bin Indicators, log spacing*

case, the model was trained to predict the general type of action that the driver would perform next. We started with 40 feature groups. Performance improves until there are only a few feature groups remaining. In this case the remaining feature groups were, in decreasing order of information content: Whether the car had arrived at the destination, The elapsed time from the start of the trip to setting the destination, The current distance to the destination, The total distance of traffic jams on the current route, Whether the current day was a weekday, The motion status of the car (driving, paused, or stopped), and The user's current preference for the type of route to be selected by the navigation system. Our proposed method of feature selection improved prediction performance from 93.0% to 94.1% when predicting the general type of the next action performed. Although this is a preliminary result based on scripted data, the prediction accuracy is promising and the most relevant features after feature selection are in general intuitively related to driver behavior.

2.4. Interface Augmentation using predictions

Several different kinds of dynamic modifications to the car HMI are possible based on prediction of what the user's next actions will be. Active modifications include removing or reordering choices in the standard HMI menus (graphic or dialog state). We have some concerns about this kind of modification, as this can result in a mismatch between the user's mental model of the system and the actual system behavior, which can lead to user confusion or stress. It is also possible to have a more passive interface affordance which is a dynamic overlay of suggested actions in addition to the fixed set of HMI menus. This preserves the match between the user's mental model and the system, while still providing a set of shortcuts that the user can choose when they correspond to a desired action. Anytime one of the shortcuts is correct, the number of actions needed to complete the task will be reduced, thus reducing task completion time.

Algorithm 1 Feature Selection for a set S of n feature groups

procedure SELECTFEATURES(S)
  $L \leftarrow []$
  $best\_acc \leftarrow 0$
  $least\_useful \leftarrow None$
  $R \leftarrow S$ ▷ R is the set of remaining feature groups
  while $\|R\| \geq 0$ **do**
    for g in R **do** ▷ g is a group of related features
      $R' \leftarrow R - g$
      $m \leftarrow train\_model(R')$
      $acc \leftarrow eval\_model(m)$
      if $acc \geq best\_acc$ **then** $least\_useful \leftarrow g$
      end if
    end for
    $L \leftarrow L.append(least\_useful)$
    $R \leftarrow R - least\_useful$
  end while
  return L ▷ L is the list of feature groups
end procedure

3. PREDICTION OF DRIVER INTENTION FROM THE DRIVER SPEECH

This section describes the prediction of driver intention from the driver speech based on a neural network classifier. Let $g \in \mathcal{G}$ be a classification category with a classification set $\mathcal{G}$, which can be either goal or intention. The prediction is formulated as the following multiple output classification problem:

$$\hat{g} = \arg\max_{g \in \mathcal{G}} p(g|\mathcal{X}). \quad (2)$$

$p(g|\mathcal{X})$ is a posterior distribution given word sequences (ASR outputs) $\mathcal{X} = \{X(1), X(2), \ldots, X(i), \ldots, X(T)\}$ in a speech utterance/dialog, where $X(i) \in \{0,1\}^{|\mathcal{W}|}$ is a one-hot word vector at word position i. T is the number of words in a sequence. The number of dimensions $|\mathcal{W}|$ corresponds to the vocabulary size (the number of distinct words) in vocabulary $\mathcal{W}$. One of the issues for this classification is that $\mathcal{X}$ is a variable-length vector sequence in an utterance or a dialog, and we need to deal with this property in the classification framework. Conventional intention and goal estimation approaches use the bag of word (BOW) feature, $X_{BOW} \in \mathbb{R}^{|\mathcal{W}|}$ (or bag of intention features in goal estimation) as fixed-dimension vector inputs, i.e.,

$$\hat{g} = \arg\max_{g \in \mathcal{G}} p(g|X_{BOW}). \quad (3)$$

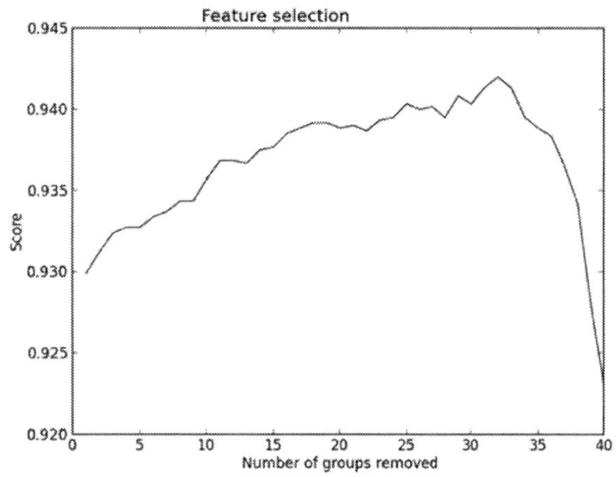

Fig. 3. *Feature selection - accuracy as feature groups are removed*

We use multivariate logistic regression to compute $P(g|X_{BOW})$ for classification target g and feature vector X_{BOW} as

$$P(g|X_{BOW}) = \text{softmax}([W_{BOW}X_{BOW}]_g), \quad (4)$$

where $[X]_g$ means a g-th raw element of vector X. $W_{BOW} \in \mathbb{R}^{|\mathcal{G}|\times|\mathcal{W}|}$ is a weight matrix to be estimated at the training step. The softmax function softmax$(\cdot)$ is defined as follows

$$\text{softmax}(z_m) \triangleq \frac{e^{z_m}}{\sum_n e^{z_n}} \quad (5)$$

Thus, once we obtain the fixed-length vector representation (X_{BOW} in the BOW feature case), the method provides a posterior distribution of the classification category, which can predict intention or goal.

However, one of the problems of applying BOW features to SLU tasks is that the feature vector tends to be very sparse. Each utterance only includes a dozen words at most unlike document analysis. Therefore, the feature vector sometimes lacks enough semantic information to accurately estimate user intentions or goals. This section first investigates the use of additional semantic information by using word embedding [12] and latent topic model based on Latent Dirichlet Allocation (LDA) [13] techniques for intention understanding and goal estimation.

3.1. Incorporating Semantic information

In this section, we import semantic text embeddings to our SLU tasks. Two kinds of semantic features are trained in unsupervised fashion using large-scale web data. One is a word-level embedding which learns contextual information about word sequences by a feed-forward neural network. The other is document-level topic embedding, which models the latent topic information of a given sentence or article. The two kinds of semantic features have respective advantages: word-level embedding captures local contextual information, while topic embedding capture the statistics of the corpus, and thus provides more global information. Then, we extracted an augmented feature $X_{LDA} \in \mathbb{R}^K$ from LDA and $X_w \in \mathbb{R}^J$ from word embedding, where K is the number of latent topics in LDA and J is the number of dimensions in an embedded space. Note that $|\mathcal{W}| > K$ or J. Thus, the classification problem in Eq. (3) can be extended as:

$$\hat{g} = \arg\max_{g\in\mathcal{G}} p(g|[X_{BOW}^\top, X_{LDA}^\top, X_w^\top]^\top). \quad (6)$$

Augmented vectors X_{LDA} and X_w provide the dense features in addition to the BOW based sparse features, which contributes to improve the classification performance.

3.1.1. Word embedding

Many current NLP systems use a bag-of-words or one-hot word vector as an input, which leads to feature vectors of extremely large dimension. An alternative is a word embedding, which projects the large sparse ($|\mathcal{W}|$) word feature vector into a low-dimensional ($J < |\mathcal{W}|$), dense vector representation.

There are two main model families for learning word vectors: 1) matrix factorization methods, such as latent semantic analysis (LSA) [14] and 2) neural network language model (NNLM) based methods, which model on local context window, such as Continuous Bag of Words (CBOW), Skip-gram [12]. The Skip-gram predicts surrounding words given the current word $X(i)$, as follows:

$$p(X(i-L),\ldots X(i-1), X(i+1),\ldots, X(i+L)|X(i)). \quad (7)$$

$X(i-L),\ldots X(i-1), X(i+1),\ldots, X(i+L)$ are $2L$ surrounding word contexts, which will be predicted in the skip gram framework. This can be estimated by one-hidden layer neural network, and the first liner transformation matrix $\phi \in K \times |\mathcal{W}|$ corresponds to embed high-dimensional ($|\mathcal{W}|$) one-hot vector to the low dimensional (J) dense vector, i.e.,

$$X_w(i) = \phi X(i). \quad (8)$$

Then for each turn or sentence, X_w is obtained by summing over normalized embedded word vectors for each word in the turn or sentence:

$$\bar{X}_w = \sum_{i\in\{1..T\}} \frac{X_w(i)}{||X_w(i)||} \quad (9)$$

$\bar{X}_w$ is used in Eq. (6) as an augmented feature vector, instead of unnormalized feature X_w.

Mikolov's toolkit 'word2vec' which implement Skip-gram and CBOW can train on large-scale corpora very efficiently. Therefore, in this paper, we used word2vec to train

Skip-gram and CBOW on a large scale web corpus collected from the internet and chose the embedding that gave the best SLU performance. The typical word usage in our route guidance task differs from web texts, so we expected that fine-tuning of the word embedding would yield additional performance improvements by adapting the word embedding model to our target task.

3.1.2. Latent topic models

Latent topic models are algorithms that can discover semantic information from a collection of documents. Topic embedding, widely used in information retrieval, treats a document as a mixture of topics and uses a vector to represent the topic distribution. Classic latent topic models have been used for SLU including Probabilistic Latent Semantic Analysis (PLSA) [15] and LDA [13]. Most latent variable models are generative models, which therefore can be used in unsupervised fashion. The latent topic model provides the posterior probability $p(k|X_{BOW})$ for each topic given (BOW) feature X_{BOW}, which is used as the kth element of an augmented LDA feature vector X_{LDA}, i.e.,

$$[X_{LDA}]_k = p(k|X_{BOW}), \tag{10}$$

The augmented feature X_{LDA} is also used in Eq. (6). However, since LDA embedding is obtained an iterative inference algorithm (variational EM) or sampling method, it is hard to fine-tune an LDA embedding within a neural network framework. Therefore, in this paper, we do not fine-tune LDA features. It could be possible to use a deep unfolding method to fine-tune the LDA inference, such as that presented in [16].

3.2. Fine-tuning of linear input networks

The previous section applies the semantic information as input features. This section uses them as an additional input layer in neural network architectures, by following the great success of neural network approaches in various SLU tasks with pre-training [17]. In applying these techniques to SLU, one major difficulty is that we often have insufficient training data for a task, since the annotation of collected data can be expensive. The performance of a neural network trained in low resource conditions is usually inferior because of overtraining. Our approach uses word embedding as an additional input layer of a neural network, which mitigates the overtraining problem. To accomplish this, we initialize the affine transformation of the first layer by using a word embedding matrix estimated from a large-scale general corpus with unsupervised training methods (pre-training). Then, the entire SLU network is trained with the annotated training data, with word embeddings fine-tuned to the SLU task. This concept has been studied in [8, 18], and the following section also describes the pre-training idea by employing word embedding framework.

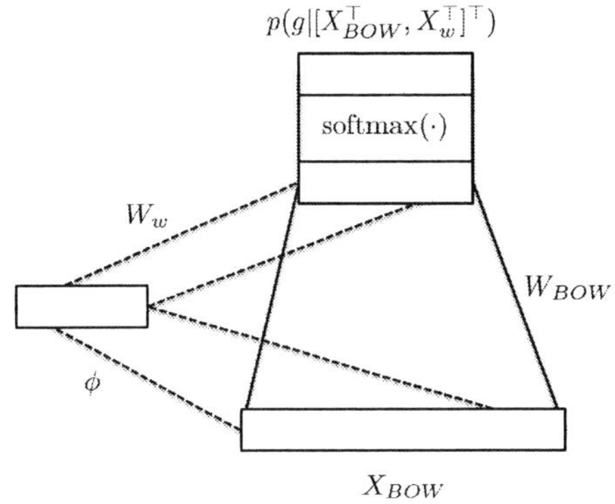

Fig. 4. *Two-layer feed-forward architecture of goal/intention prediction network with pre-training based on ϕ.*

3.2.1. Feed-forward architecture

We start from Eq. (6) without the LDA feature X_{LDA}. By using the logistic regression equation (Eq. (4)), the posterior distribution $p(g|[X_{BOW}^\top, X_w^\top]^\top)$ can be rewritten as the two matrix multiplication for input features X_{BOW} and X_w as follows:

$$\begin{aligned} &p(g|[X_{BOW}^\top, X_w^\top]^\top) \\ &\quad = \text{softmax}([W_{BOW}X_{BOW} + W_w X_w]_g), \end{aligned} \tag{11}$$

where $W_w \in \mathbb{R}^{|\mathcal{G}|\times J}$ is a weight matrix. Let X_w be obtained as an unnormalized vector of Eq. (9), i.e., $X_w = \sum_{i\in\{1..T\}} X_w(i)$, Eq. (11) is rewritten with Eq. (8), as follows:

$$\begin{aligned} &p(g|[X_{BOW}^\top, X_w^\top]^\top) \\ &\quad = \text{softmax}([W_{BOW}X_{BOW} + W_w\phi X_{BOW}]_g) \\ &\quad = \text{softmax}([(W_{BOW} + W_w\phi)\,X_{BOW}]_g) \end{aligned} \tag{12}$$

Thus, we can regard Eq. (12) as a two-layer neural network given input feature X_{BOW}. That is, the feed-forward architecture changes the baseline structure by adding a linear hidden layer between the Bag-of-Words input layer and the output layer (as Figure 4). The posterior probability of the goal/intention given the input features is calculated through the final softmax layer. Although the proposed architecture has three weight matrices ϕ, W_{BOW}, and W_w, ϕ can be initialized from the word embedding matrix (pre-training), and we can efficiently estimate these matrices. Note that the goal estimation task uses several utterances as an input feature, and our experiments use utterance-wise feature X_I. We use the N-best intention confidence score obtained by the other intention estimation module than that described in this paper as X_I.

3.2.2. *Multi-scale recurrent neural network (MSRNN)*

The limitation of the above methods is that we do not explicitly deal with a sequential property. This can be performed by using RNN. By considering the dialog structure based on multiple scale property based on word and utterance unit, we also propose a novel Multi-Scale RNN (MSRNN) architecture pre-trained with word embedding in order to capture long-term characteristics over the entire dialog for goal estimation. The proposed MSRNN uses two sub-networks to model the different time scales represented by word and turn sequences.

The goal estimation task has two input sequences for each sample: a word sequence $\mathcal{X} = \{X(1), \ldots, X(i), \ldots, X(T)\}$ and an utterance sequence $\mathcal{I} = \{I(1), \ldots, I(j), \ldots, I(M)\}$. The two sequences have different time scales, and $T > M$. However, the baseline architecture treats word input as bag-of-words, which ignores the contextual information of the input. Both input sequences, word and intention, contain contextual information, and intuitively a system that captures this information may perform better than one which does not. Therefore, the proposed MSRNN architecture can model the different time scales represented by word and intention sequences, shown in Figure 5.

The lower half of this figure represents the short time scale RNN, which accepts feature vectors for words $X(i)$ in all history utterances, as an entire sequence. The recurrent connection is represented as follows:

$$h_x(i) = \text{sigmoid}(\phi_x X(i) + W_x h_w(i-1)), \qquad (13)$$

where we use the element-wise sigmoid function at the hidden layer defined as:

$$\text{sigmoid}(x) = \frac{1}{1+e^{-x}}. \qquad (14)$$

W_x and ϕ_x are weight matrices of recurrent connection and word embedding, respectively. ϕ_x is initialized by a word embedding matrix, similar to the discussion in the previous section, and the back propagation through time is used to fine-tune ϕ_x.

The upper half of the figure represents the long time scale RNN, which accepts a single intention feature vector $I(j)$ for each utterance, and use all intentions in history as a sequence. The recurrent connection is represented as follows:

$$h_I(j) = \text{sigmoid}(\phi_I I(j) + W_I h_I(j-1)). \qquad (15)$$

W_I and ϕ_I are also weight matrices of recurrent connection and word embedding, respectively. The upper RNN has longer sequence than lower RNN. The two RNN structures have different parameters and are jointly trained. The goal is predicted at the end of each turn, and the last hidden vector of word sequence $h_x(T)$ and last hidden vector of intention sequence $h_I(M)$ are concatenated to predict the output layer

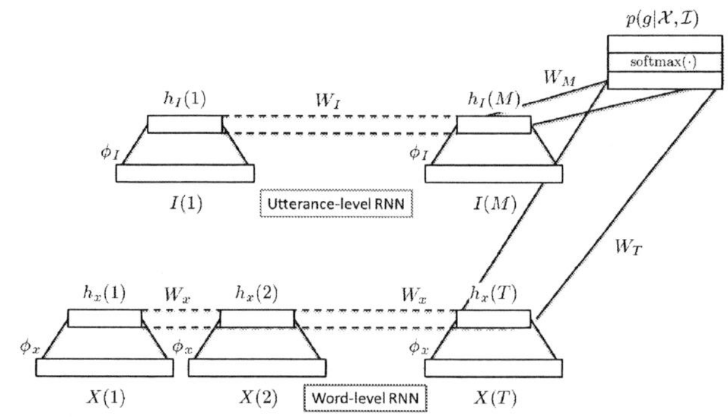

Fig. 5. *Multi-scale recurrent neural network (MSRNN) composed of utterance and word level RNNs*

(goal of the current turn), i.e.,

$$p(g|\mathcal{X},\mathcal{I}) = \text{softmax}(W_T h_x(T) + W_M h_I(M) + b) \quad (16)$$

where W_T, W_M, and b are weight matrices and bias vector, respectively, which combine the long and short time scale RNNs. ϕ_I, W_x, W_I, W_M, W_T, and b are randomly initialized, unlike ϕ_x.

3.3. Experiments

We built and tested models using data from a Japanese route guidance spoken dialog system. We used a 1.8G Japanese web text corpus from the Internet to train word2vec, and the full Japanese Wikipedia (900k documents) to train LDA. Combination of 50, 100, 150, and 300 word2vec dimensions, and 50, 100 LDA dimensions were tested. The dimensionality with the best result was selected. All text was tokenized and morpholized first by a Japanese morpholizer, ChaSen. For each word, we use the word, pronunciation, and part of speech as individual token elements. Each token is in Word+Pronunciation+POS format. For both Japanese web data and Wikipedia data, low frequency words (frequency < 5) are replaced by UNKNOWN token. The total reduced vocabulary is around 150k.

3.3.1. *Intention understanding*

We evaluated the performance of fine-tuning on the intention understanding task. We collected a database of Japanese utterances in an automobile scenario with annotated intentions, which contains 39,328 training samples, 5,000 dev samples and 5,000 test samples. The number of intention categories is 562, and the vocabulary size is 3,602. Each sentence is represented as a Bag-of-Words feature vector. We tested the performance of word2vec features by concatenating the 300-dimensional word2vec features with the Bag-of-Words features, and additionally tested the system both with and without fine-tuning.

Table 1. Average error rate for intention prediction task, (ft) means with fine-tuning

	Dev (%)	Test (%)
Baseline (Bag-of-Words)	15.7	15.9
BOW + word2vec	13.0	13.5
BOW + word2vec (ft)	12.4	12.3

Table 2. Average error rate for goal estimation task, (ft) means with fine-tuning

	Dev (%)	Test (%)
Baseline (intention only)	18.9	19.5
intention (100 dim) + word2vec (50 dim)	17.2	17.5
intention (100 dim) + word2vec (50 dim + ft)	16.0	16.1
intention (100 dim) + word2vec (50 dim + ft) + LDA (50)	16.0	16.2

The experimental results are shown in Table 1. By using the word2vec features, the performance was improved from the baseline system by 2.7% (dev.) and 2.4% (eval) (absolute reduction in error). With the fine-tuning, the performance further improves to 3.3% (dev.) and 3.6% (eval), absolutely. This result confirms the effectiveness of fine-tuning for our intention understanding task.

3.3.2. Goal estimation

We collected a dataset from a Japanese rule-based spoken dialog system, which contain 7059 turns in total. The log data contains the Japanese ASR results, system prompts, estimated N-best intentions, system actions, and an annotated goal for each turn. The intention vector consists of a sparse vector concatenated by N-best intentions (545 dimensions) and N-best system actions (545 dimensions). The dimension for user intention and system action together is 1090, the dimension for goal is 544 in total. Since the data size was very limited, we split the data into 4 folds, $3/4$ used for training, $1/8$ for validation and $1/8$ for test respectively. To evaluate the performance of our proposed approaches, we used the average accuracy across the 4 folds. We compared the result of using embeddings alone versus embeddings with fine-tuning. In the RNN architecture, hidden layer sizes of 100, 200 and 300 for the intention RNN module were trained and the one with best result was selected (100 for both with and without fine tuning). The model was trained by stochastic gradient descent.

We observe from Table 2 that importing semantic text features gives a better performance than using intention features alone. The best performance occurs on smaller semantic embedding dimensions and smaller hidden layer dimensions. The reason for this is due to the limited data size, for which fine-tuning high dimensional embeddings could lead to overtraining problems.

Fine-tuning word embeddings improves upon the feature engineering results by a small but consistent margin. The first four rows of the table are implemented by the feed-forward structure and the last two rows are implemented by the MSRNN structure. Among all the feed-forward structures, fine-tuning word2vec plus LDA features gives the best result with 2.9% (dev.) and 3.3% (eval.) absolute improvement from the baseline. The MSRNN structure itself (without fine-tuning) already gives a significant performance improvement over simply importing semantic text features. When we add fine-tuning to the MSRNN training, we get the best overall result of 3.3% (dev.) and 3.6% (eval.) absolute improvement from the baseline. This proves that modeling time sequential input by using our MSRNN architecture with different time scales gives a gain to the system.

4. CONCLUSIONS

This paper investigates the use of driver action prediction through 1) the driver interaction with the car HMI based on the driving history and 2) in-vehicle dialog systems based on SLU. The first topic focuses on the processing and selection of data features from the driving history, followed by feature selection to improve prediction performance. The second topic improved the prediction performance of user intention and goal estimation tasks based on a novel recurrent neural network.

In both cases we showed the feasibility of predicting the driver's actions, even from training with a small dataset. Future development of this work will involve using these predictions to improve the car HMI, and evaluating the effect on task completion rates and completion times. Also, we expect that further work on issues of sparse data will be needed: both methods rely on machine learning techniques and currently require large amounts of data to obtain robust performance.

5. REFERENCES

[1] S. G. Klauer, T. A. Dingus, V. L. Neale, J. D. Sudweeks, and D. J. Ramsey, "The impact of driver inattention on

near-crash/crash risk: An analysis using the 100-car naturalistic driving study data," tech. rep., 2006.

[2] D. D. Salvucci, D. Markley, M. Zuber, and D. P. Brumby, "ipod distraction: Effects of portable music-player use on driver performance," in *Proceedings of the SIGCHI conference on Human factors in computing systems*, pp. 243–250, ACM, 2007.

[3] L. Garay-Vega, A. Pradhan, G. Weinberg, B. Schmidt-Nielsen, B. Harsham, Y. Shen, G. Divekar, M. Romoser, M. Knodler, and D. Fisher, "Evaluation of different speech and touch interfaces to in-vehicle music retrieval systems," *Accident analysis & prevention*, vol. 42, no. 3, pp. 913–920, 2010.

[4] N. H. T. S. Administration *et al.*, "Visual-manual nhtsa driver distraction guidelines for in-vehicle electronic devices," *Washington, DC: National Highway Traffic Safety Administration (NHTSA), Department of Transportation (DOT)*, 2012.

[5] D. Jurafsky and J. H. Martin, *Speech & Language Processing*. Pearson Education, 2000.

[6] R. De Mori, "Spoken language understanding: a survey.," in *Proceedings of IEEE Automatic Speech Recognition and Understanding Workshop (ASRU)*, pp. 365–376, 2007.

[7] R. Sarikaya, G. E. Hinton, and A. Deoras, "Application of deep belief networks for natural language understanding," *IEEE/ACM Transactions on Audio, Speech and Language Processing*, vol. 22, no. 4, pp. 778–784, 2014.

[8] G. Mesnil, X. He, L. Deng, and Y. Bengio, "Investigation of recurrent-neural-network architectures and learning methods for spoken language understanding," in *Proceedings of Interspeech*, 2013.

[9] K. Yao, B. Peng, G. Zweig, D. Yu, X. Li, and F. Gao, "Recurrent conditional random field for language understanding," in *Proceedings of IEEE International Conference on Acoustics, Speech and Signal Processing (ICASSP)*, pp. 4077–4081, IEEE, 2014.

[10] Y. Luan, S. Watanabe, and B. Harsham, "Efficient learning for spoken language understanding tasks with word embedding based pre-training," in *Proceedings of the Interspeech*, 2015.

[11] F. Pedregosa, G. Varoquaux, A. Gramfort, V. Michel, B. Thirion, O. Grisel, M. Blondel, P. Prettenhofer, R. Weiss, V. Dubourg, J. Vanderplas, A. Passos, D. Cournapeau, M. Brucher, M. Perrot, and E. Duchesnay, "Scikit-learn: Machine learning in Python," *Journal of Machine Learning Research*, vol. 12, pp. 2825–2830, 2011.

[12] T. Mikolov, K. Chen, G. Corrado, and J. Dean, "Efficient estimation of word representations in vector space," *arXiv preprint arXiv:1301.3781*, 2013.

[13] D. M. Blei, A. Y. Ng, and M. I. Jordan, "Latent dirichlet allocation," *the Journal of Machine Learning Research*, vol. 3, pp. 993–1022, 2003.

[14] S. C. Deerwester, S. T. Dumais, T. K. Landauer, G. W. Furnas, and R. A. Harshman, "Indexing by latent semantic analysis," *the Journal of the American Society of Information Science*, vol. 41, no. 6, pp. 391–407, 1990.

[15] T. Hofmann, "Probabilistic latent semantic indexing," in *Proceedings of the 22nd annual international ACM SIGIR conference on Research and development in information retrieval*, pp. 50–57, ACM, 1999.

[16] J. R. Hershey, J. L. Roux, and F. Weninger, "Deep unfolding: Model-based inspiration of novel deep architectures," *arXiv preprint arXiv:1409.2574*, 2014.

[17] G. Hinton, L. Deng, D. Yu, G. E. Dahl, A. Mohamed, N. Jaitly, A. Senior, V. Vanhoucke, P. Nguyen, T. N. Sainath, and B. Kingsbury, "Deep neural networks for acoustic modeling in speech recognition: The shared views of four research groups," *IEEE Signal Processing Magazine*, vol. 29, no. 6, pp. 82–97, 2012.

[18] X. Song, X. He, J. Gao, and L. Deng, "Unsupervised learning of word semantic embedding using the deep structured semantic model," Tech. Rep. MSR-TR-2014-109, August 2014.

Improvement by Adding Video Feature in an Acoustic Ambiance Simulation for Automobiles

Alankar Warhadpande[1], Christian Lüke[1], Anne Theiß[1], Gerhard Schmidt[1]

[1]: Digital Signal Processing and System Theory, University of Kiel, Germany
E-mail: alwa@tf.uni-kiel.de, cl@tf.uni-kiel.de, ath@tf.uni-kiel.de

Abstract In this paper we demonstrate how the combination of acoustical and visual stimuli can be introduced in an ambiance simulation for automobiles. The synchronization of the audio and the video is very important and is discussed in this paper. Furthermore, a subjective evaluation was performed which proved that the combined presentation of acoustical and visual stimuli is more effective than a separate presentation of audio or video. Ten participants were shown seventeen different scenarios. At the time of the evaluation some questions were asked to measure how realistic the ambiance is. Most of the participants felt that the combined audio-visual ambiance simulation is most effective. This result also shows that the audio-visual simulation has a significant effect for creating a realistic ambiance for automobiles.

Keywords ambiance simulation, virtual environment, immersion, subjective testing

1. INTRODUCTION

Nowadays, varieties of vehicles are continuously increasing in the market and also the customers expectations .With the help of research and development automobile industries are trying to meet the increasing requirements with respect to quality and comfort [1]. Visual driving simulators are used in automotive research and industry to prove new systems and evaluate the driver's behavior and interactions with the vehicle. The visual driving simulators combine haptic, visual, and acoustic cues in order to immerse the driver into a sufficient degree of realism [2]. The effectiveness of these simulators depends largely on how efficiently they recreate the real world [3]. These driving simulators are helpful because their versatility helps to reduce the cost of new developments. By covering various situations and scenarios, problems can be detected and eliminated and thus the vehicle safety can be increased. It also plays a significant role in evaluating vehicle designs [4]. Finally, all sorts of experiments can be performed repeatedly under controlled conditions.

2. ACOUSTIC AMBIANCE SIMULATION

In the university of Kiel, an acoustic ambiance simulation with emphasis on driving simulation has been implemented [2]. The aim of the acoustic ambiance simulation is to recreate any desired noise scenario within a sound-proof room or within a vehicle. The simulation can be used to record clean speech in a realistic noise environment. This is achieved by generating orthogonal loudspeaker signals that can be canceled from the microphone signals.

2.1. Audio Recordings

In order to generate a reference for the simulation, the desired noise scenario has to be recorded at first. The signals have been obtained using calibrated microphones at specified reference positions, e.g. using in-ear microphones or microphones at the car's built-in microphone positions. The short-term Fourier transforms of these reference signals originating from a real environment will be referred to as *reference microphone* (short-term) spectra $R_m(\mu, k)$, where m is the microphone index, μ the subband index, and k the frame index.

These spectra are used to feed the loudspeaker signal generation. This can be implemented either by a simple assignment of microphone signals to loudspeakers (e.g., left ear microphone signal to left loudspeaker), or using beamforming techniques. The result will be referred to as *template loudspeaker* spectra $\check{X}_l(\mu, k)$.

The spectra received by the microphones while reproducing the scenario are referred to as *auxiliary microphone* (short-term) spectra $Y_m(\mu, k)$. It is important that the microphones are calibrated prior to both the recording and the equalization.

2.2. Creation of Loudspeaker Signals

In a first step, all signals are transformed into frequency domain by applying an overlap-add-based analysis filterbank. Then, white noise is generated in the short-term frequency domain for each loudspeaker and in each subband using a linear congruential generator $\mathcal{N}$,

$$X_l^{\text{wn}}(\mu, k) = \begin{cases} \mathcal{N}, & \text{if } \mu = 0 \text{ or } \mu = N_{\text{Sbb}} - 1, \\ \frac{\mathcal{N} + j \cdot \mathcal{N}}{\sqrt{2}}, & \text{else.} \end{cases} \tag{1}$$

The generated noise is first equalized by applying real-valued gains $g_l(\mu)$ and modulated using time-varying factors $\xi_l(\mu, k)$

in each frequency band μ,

$$X_l(\mu, k) \;=\; g_l(\mu)\, \xi_l(\mu, k)\, X_l^{\text{wn}}(\mu, k). \tag{2}$$

The modulation factors $\xi_l(\mu, k)$ are calculated from the modulation of the template loudspeaker spectra,

$$\xi_l(\mu, k) = \frac{|\check{X}_l(\mu, k)|}{\frac{1}{K}\sum_{\kappa=0}^{K-1} |\check{X}_l(\mu, \kappa)|}, \tag{3}$$

where K is the length of the scenario in frames. An equalization procedure assures that the power spectral densities are reproduced correctly at the reference positions. In this case, the reference positions are the ears of the listening subject. A linear optimization finds the weights $g_l(\mu)$ such that

$$E = \sum_{m=0}^{M-1} \sum_{\mu=0}^{N_{\text{Sbb}}-1} \sum_{k=0}^{K-1} \Big(|R_m(\mu, k)| - |Y_m(\mu, k)| \Big)^2 \tag{4}$$

is minimized, where M is the number of microphones, N_{Sbb} is the number of subbands, and K is the length of the scenario to be calibrated in frames. The optimization also contains the inequality condition

$$\mathrm{E}\Big\{ |X_l(\mu, k)|^2 \Big\} < X_{\max}^2 \tag{5}$$

that the subband loudspeaker power $\mathrm{E}\left\{|X_l(\mu, k)|^2\right\}$ must not exceed a certain threshold $X_{\max}^2$. If the weights $g_l(\mu)$ change too quickly over frequency, strong spatial comb-filter effects may appear. This observation lead to an extension of the optimization criterion,

$$E' = E + \gamma \sum_{l=0}^{L-1} \sum_{\mu=0}^{N_{\text{Sbb}}-1} (g_l(\mu) - \overline{g}_l)^2, \tag{6}$$

where $\overline{g}_l = \frac{1}{N_{\text{Sbb}}} \sum_{\mu=0}^{N_{\text{Sbb}}-1} g_l(\mu)$. The parameter γ controls the balance of the flatness of the frequency response on the one hand and the equalization performance on the other hand.

3. VISUAL AMBIANCE SIMULATION

In this section, the implementation of video in the acoustic ambiance simulation is explained along with the method to synchronize the recorded audio and video. The aim is to develop a video player which plays and repeats the recorded video without any gap and also synchronizes the audio and the video.

3.1. Video Recordings

During a real drive, a video was recorded from the 'front passengers' point of view using a professional video camera (Sony FDR-AX100E). Different recording angles were tried and assessed to get an optimal result in the playback situation.

The drive recordings were done in the city and on highways with different speeds such as stand-still, 50km/h, 100km/h, 130km/h, and 190km/h.

3.2. Video Player

The features which are needed by the video player are:

- repeat a video without any delay (gap-less A-B repeat),
- seek to a certain position without any delay,
- hide the video (for evaluation purposes), and
- synchronize the recorded audio and video.

The gap-less A-B repeat enables to show a part of the recording repeatedly, giving the impression of a long, continuous video. This is necessary if the simulated scenario is of a longer duration than the recording, which easily happens especially when simulating high speeds.

For the playback of a scenario it is usually necessary to play back a part of the video recording which does not start at the beginning of the recorded file. To let the playback start quickly, the video player should seek to that file position with as little delay as possible. Depending on the video codec, all frames since the last key frame have to be rendered before the video playback can start. Taking all these features into consideration a video player was built using C++ and Qt.

3.3. Synchronization

While the video is recorded by a video camera, the binaural audio signals are recorded by an eight-channel sound card using Shure MX-183 microphones. Because the separate recordings can not be triggered at exactly the same time, a synchronization of the audio and the video is required. Furthermore, the clock of the camera and of the sound card can not easily be synchronized, which might result in slightly different sample rates. In order to synchronize video and audio, a cross-correlation analysis of the binaural sound recordings $x(n)$ on the one hand and the audio track $v(n)$ of the video recording on the other hand is performed,

$$r_{xv}(\nu) = \mathrm{E}\left\{x(n)\, v(n+\nu)\right\}. \tag{7}$$

As the recorded signals have a duration of up to one hour, the signals need to be divided into blocks of several minutes. The cross-correlation analysis is then performed for each block b of length L,

$$\hat{r}_{xv}^{b}(\nu) = \frac{1}{L} \sum_{n=b\,L}^{(b+1)\,L-1-|\nu|} x(n)\, v(n+\nu). \tag{8}$$

Figure 1 shows the cross-correlation estimate $\hat{r}^0_{xv}(\nu)$ of the first block. In this case, the recording of the audio was started 96 s after the video. The estimated lag $\hat{\lambda}^b$ is then chosen as the maximum argument of the absolute cross-correlation estimate,

$$\hat{\lambda}^b = \underset{\nu \in \{0,\ldots,L-1\}}{\arg\max} \left\{ |\hat{r}^b_{xv}(\nu)| \right\}. \tag{9}$$

Figure 2 shows the estimated lag value $\hat{\lambda}^b$ of each block b. If the measured lags between video and audio stay the same for all blocks, i.e.,

$$|\hat{\lambda} - \hat{\lambda}^b| < \epsilon \quad \forall b \quad \text{with} \quad \hat{\lambda} = \frac{1}{B}\sum_{b=1}^{B} \hat{\lambda}^b, \tag{10}$$

then the sample rates of the sound card and of the camera can be assumed to be the same. This is the case, as can be seen in Figure 2. The estimated lag for the presented recording was $\hat{\lambda} = 95.96$ s. An increase or decrease of the measured lags from one block to the next indicates that the clocks of the video camera and the audio soundcard differ slightly. If professional recording hardware was being used, this can be prevented by synchronizing the video camera and the soundcard using a clock synchronization cable. Otherwise, the video frame rate could be slightly adapted or a resampling of the audio files could be performed.

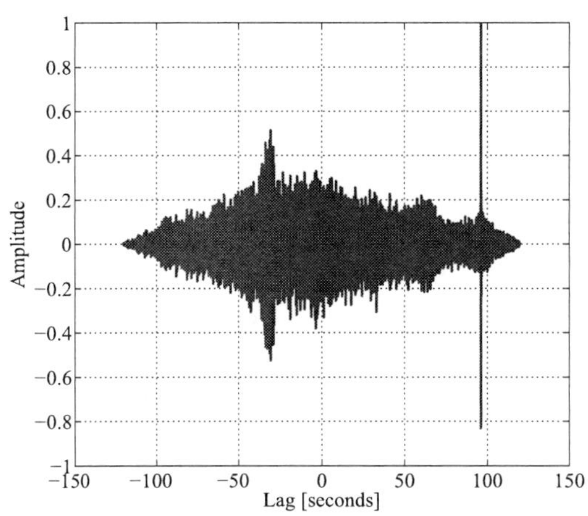

Fig. 1. Cross correlation of the first block.

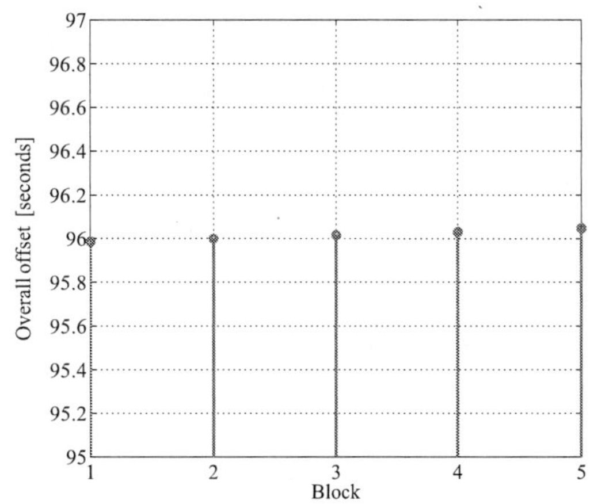

Fig. 2. Lag value of each block.

4. EVALUATION

4.1. Participants

10 volunteers participated in the evaluation. Out of 10 volunteers, 1 was female and 9 were males. The participants were aged between 24 and 35 years with an average age of 27 years. Because the questions asked during the evaluation were related to driving, all participants needed to be driving license holders.

4.2. Design

A Mercedes S-class test car was used for the purpose of evaluation. Custom-built loudspeakers were attached to the car windows to create the acoustic ambiance. The car was placed in front of a big projection screen. An LCD projector was used to play the video on the screen to create the visual ambiance. Figure 3 shows the design of the driving simulator.

Fig. 3. Design of the Audio-Visual Ambiance Simulator.

4.3. Scenarios

Recordings were done at five different speeds (0 km/h, 50 km/h, 100 km/h, 130 km/h, and 190 km/h). For each speed, three scenarios were created, one consisting of audio only,

Fig. 4. A view from inside of the Audio-Visual Ambiance Simulator.

Fig. 5. Acoustic ambiance simulation using window loudspeakers inside our test car.

one of video only, and one of audio plus video.With these combinations fifteen scenarios were generated. These fifteen scenarios were shown in a random order. For each of these scenarios, the participants were asked to guess the speed of the car from the possible choices given in the questions and also have to rate the naturalness of the ambiance simulation.

The scenarios 16 and 17 consist of audio and video. Instead of driving at a constant speed, the recordings contain turning, stopping at a traffic light, accelerating, and changing the lane. In these scenarios, the participants were asked to tell what they feel after seeing and hearing the video and audio in a multiple-choice fashion. For example, the participants may feel to turn the steering wheel, apply the break, or accelerate the car.

Lastly some questions which are mentioned in the section below were to be answered.

4.4. Measures

In this evaluation the measures of quality and reactions to the ambiance were taken from the Swedish viewer-user presence questionnaire (SVUP) [3]. A short version of questionnaire was used which consist of 9 questions. A five-point rating scale was used where "very much" and "not at all" were the endpoints. Below is the set of questions.

- To what extent the interaction with the environment was natural?
- To what extent you were involved in the driving task?
- To what extent did you think that the things you did and saw happened naturally and without much mental effort?
- To what extent did you feel disoriented or confused in the virtual environment?
- To what extent did you focus your attention on the situation, rather than other things?
- To what extent did you find the virtual environment comfortable ?
- To what extent were you able to identify sounds?
- To what extent were you able to localize sounds?
- To what extent did you think that the video contributed to the overall realism?

4.5. Procedure

In the evaluation, the participants were asked one by one to sit in the car. Some time is given to them to get acquainted with the environment. A sample video is also shown to them just to give the participants an idea about what is going to happen in the evaluation. Three sheets of papers were given to them with the questions related to the 17 scenarios explained in the sections above.

5. RESULTS

The median of the speeds guessed by the participants is shown in Table 1. It can be seen from this table that the median is always closest to the actual driving speed when both video and audio were presented to the participants. This is an indication that the combined presence of audio and video is more effective for driving simulations than audio-only or video-only simulations.

In a next step, the root mean square error (rmse) ϵ_k between the actual speed s and the speed $g_{k,i}$ guessed by the

Table 1. Median of guessed speed by participants.

Scenario	Median		
	Audio (km/h)	Video (km/h)	Audio+Video (km/h)
0 km/h	25	0	0
50 km/h	40	40	45
100 km/h	90	80	90
130 km/h	105	100	120
190 km/h	140	140	150

participants was calculated for each scenario k with

$$\epsilon_k = \sqrt{\frac{1}{N}\sum_{i=0}^{N}(s_k - g_{k,i})^2}, \tag{11}$$

where N is the number of participants. The rmse ϵ_k becomes zero if all participants were able to guess the correct speed of a scenario k. The rmse increases as the answers of the participants start to move away from the correct speed. The rmse for each scenario is shown in Table 2. It can be seen from

Table 2. Root mean square error of guessed speeds.

Scenario	Root mean square error		
	Audio (km/h)	Video (km/h)	Audio+Video (km/h)
0 km/h	41.83	0	0
50 km/h	16.73	18.97	16.43
100 km/h	39.11	39.49	34.20
130 km/h	42.77	37.54	29.32
190 km/h	55.58	67.82	52.34

the table that the rmse is least when both audio and video are incorporated in the simulation. This again indicates that adding video to the simulation helped in enhancing the driving simulation experience.

Figure 6 shows a box plot of the evaluation results. The scenarios can be found on the x-axis, where 'A', 'V', and 'A+V' represents 'Audio', 'Video' and 'Audio plus Video', respectively. The boxes represent the lower and upper quartile, the horizontal line inside the boxes represents the median.

As mentioned above, the participants were also asked to rate the ambiance created by each scenario. The extend to which the interaction with the environment was natural was rated using a scale from 1 ("very much") to 5 ("not at all"). The mean of the answers given by the participants is shown in Table 3. From this table it can be concluded that the participants could quite well immerse into the scenarios containing both audio and video. The higher and thus worse values

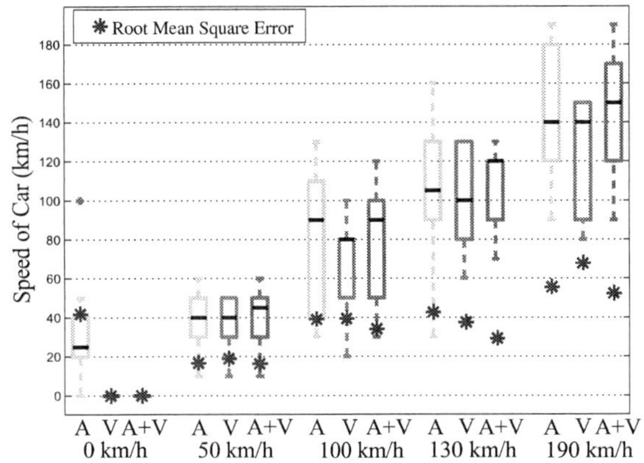

Fig. 6. Box Plot for the results of the Evaluation.

Table 3. Mean for the answer of rating the scenarios.

Scenario	Mean		
	Audio (km/h)	Video (km/h)	Audio+Video (km/h)
0 km/h	2.6	3.4	1.6
50 km/h	2.3	3.2	1.6
100 km/h	3	3.4	1.6
130 km/h	2.7	3.1	2.1
190 km/h	2.6	3.3	1.7

towards higher speeds can be explained by the shorter recordings that needed to be looped for higher speeds, resulting in frequent repetitions.

Scenarios 16 and 17, consisting of both audio and video, were created to stimulate a response from the participants as they experienced the simulation. The desired response from the participants is used as a measure of the quality of the simulator. Situations which appear to require actions such as steering, stopping, or accelerating are presented in these scenarios. In the simulation, most of the participants felt an urge to turn the steering wheel or press the brake pedal. The results of these scenarios are shown in Table 4. As it can be seen, the simulation was successful in stimulating the desired response from the participants. The participants also gave positive feedback for these scenarios when asked the feedback questions. This again demonstrates the successful enhancement of the simulator by the synchronized playback of audio and video.

6. CONCLUSIONS

The results presented above show that the audio-visual ambiance simulation is more effective than only acoustic ambiance simulation. Overall it can be observed that the participants were able to make better judgment of the speed, when

Table 4. Results of scenarios 16 and 17.

Scenario	Feeling in Scenarios	% of participants declared to feel
16	Body felt to move in direction of car	76.9
	Overtaking	46.1
17	Turn the steering wheel	46.1
	To Accelerate	61.5
	To Break	53.8
16 & 17	Dizzy	23
	Nothing	15.3

both audio and video was included in the simulation. Whenever the simulated situation seemed to require an action, most of the participants felt an urge to perform these actions.

The simulator is quite affordable as it only consists of one video screen, an LCD projector, and several loudspeakers. The simulator described and evaluated in this paper is now being used for the creation of a Lombard speech database as well as for testing In-Car-Communication systems.

In order to further improve the realism a curved screen or multiple projectors could be used so that the video covers the full eye sight of the participants sitting in the car. Furthermore, a vibration feature could be added with the help of motors attached to the wheels of the car.

7. REFERENCES

[1] Brigitte Schulte-Fortkamp, André Fiebig, Klaus Genuit, "New Approach for the Development of Vehicle Target Sounds," in *INTER-NOISE 2006*, Honolulu, Hawaii, USA 3-6 DECEMBER 2006.

[2] A. Capustiac, B. Hesse, D. Schramm, D. Banabic, "A human centered control strategy for a driving simulator," in *International Journal of Mechanical & Mechatronics Engineering*,IJMME-IJENS Vol 11 No 01, 2011.

[3] Pratik Shah, Ayman Faza,Raghavendra Nimmala, Steven Grant, William Chapin, "THE IMMERSIVE AUDIO ENVIRONMENT IMPLEMENTATION, SUBJECTIVE TESTS AND RESULTS," in *The 17th International Conference on Auditory Display (ICAD-2011)*, Budapest, Hungary, June 20-24, 2011.

[4] Norfleet, D., Wagner, J., Alexander, K., and Pidgeon, P., "Automotive Driving Simulators: Research, Education, and Entertainment," in *SAE Int. J. Passeng. Cars Electron. Electr. Syst. 2(1):186-193*, 2009, doi:10.4271/2009-01-0533.

[5] Christian Lüke, Anne Theiß, Gerhard Schmidt, Oliver Niebuhr, Tina John, "Creation of a Lombard Speech Database using an Acoustic Ambiance Simulation with Loudspeakers," in 6th *Biennial DSP Workshop for In-Vehicle Systems*, Seoul, Korea, 2013.

[6] Pontus Larsson, Daniel Västfjäll, Pierre Olsson, Mendel Kleiner, "When What You Hear is What You See: Presence and Auditory-Visual Integration in Virtual Environments," in *PRESENCE*, 2007.

Effect of speaking rate and speech complexity on transmission quality during driving navigation task

Bohan Chen[1,3,4]**, Norihide Kitaoka**[2,4]**, and Takeda Kazuya**[1,3,4]

[1]: Graduate School of Information Science, Nagoya University, Japan
[2]: Institue of Technology and Science, Tokushima University, Japan
[3]: Institute of Innovation for Future Society (MIRAI), Nagoya University, Japan
[4]: JST/COI, Japan
E-mail: {bohan.chen, takeda}@g.sp.m.is.nagoya-u.ac.jp kitaoka@is.tokushima-u.ac.jp

Abstract We investigate relationships between fixed and varying speaking rates and speech complexity on transmission quality as reflected by human speech processing and driving behavior, using a real-world, car navigation conversation corpus. We are also interested in examining conscious decisions made by human speakers to alter their normal speech patterns when interacting, and the effect this has on information transmission. Our results show that human beings tend to reduce their speaking rate when uttering complex sentences. We also found that when navigation information is provided at a fixed transmission rate, drivers exhibit better driving performance during directed driving.

Keywords information transmission, speaking rate, rational behavior, N-gram entropy

1. INTRODUCTION

Although information transmission is recognized as one of the most important goals of conversation, we have little understanding of what actually happens when information is transmitted. The goal of this study is to investigate how speaking rates and speech complexity influence information transmission quality between humans. After thousands of years of evolution, our spoken languages have likely evolved in a direction that makes information transmission faster and easier. For example, nouns in the English language at one time had one of three genders (male, female or neuter), but no longer have any gender. Words have also been combined and shortened in English, so that "motor hotel" has become "motel", and a combination of smoke and fog is now simply "smog", for example.

The relationship between a word's linguistic form and its frequency of use is an important rational property of our language, because if frequently used words have shorter linguistic forms (e.g., fewer syllables), which is the idea behind many common coding algorithms like Huffman coding, we can achieve higher average information transmission rates. Zipf noticed this relationship and expressed his empirical theory this way in 1935: "...the magnitude of words tends, on the whole, to stand in an inverse relationship to the number of occurrences" [1]. In modern times, with fast computers and high speed Internet connections, researchers have been able to verify this empirical theory by collecting statistics from the huge language corpus of the World Wide Web [2]. Moreover, rather than observing a single word's frequency of use, many researchers find that the average entropy of a word's n-gram structure, which can be described as its frequency of use within a sequence of words, has a stronger correlation with a word's linguistic importance [3].

As much of the research mentioned above is based on text analysis, in this study we focus instead on the linguistic forms of words, and investigate the relationship between the syllable level speaking rate, which is a more suitable language characteristic due to our spoken language theme, and the average syllable level entropy of a word's bi-gram structure. If spoken language has similar rational properties as written language, we should see an inverse relationship between speaking rate and sentence complexity.

A reasonable corollary of the inverse relationship between speaking rate and bi-gram structure entropy is that, as we reduce our speaking rate when presenting a high entropy message, our average information transmission rate, which has $bits/s$ as its unit, should show a tendency toward flatness or evenness. Our preference for a flat or uniform information transmission rate (also referred to as "uniform information density") has also been a target of research. In [4], speaker preferences were analyzed using a spontaneous speech corpus, and it was found that information density was an important predictor of speaker preferences during speech production. Therefore, in this study we wish to further investigate whether this preference for flat information density can help improving information transmission efficiency, and if the answer is "yes", we also want to determine if there is an optimal rate for information transmission, which can be used to achieve the highest possible information transmission efficiency.

Thus, the research questions which guide this study are as follows:

- What is the relationship between speaking rate and

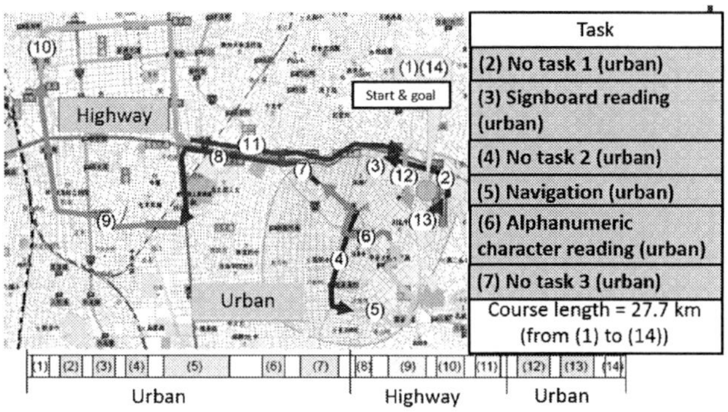

Fig. 1. Driving course for car navigation conversation corpus. Note that in this study we only used the section from (2) to (7) for our analysis.

speech complexity?

- Is there a difference in information transmission efficiency between speech presented at a fixed information transmission rate and speech presented at a variable transmission rate?

This paper is organized as follows. After a brief introduction to the car navigation dialog corpus used in this study in Section 2, we describe the measurement techniques we used in Section 3. In Section 4 we report our experimental results and discuss the implications of our results. We end the paper with our conclusions and a discussion of our future research.

2. CAR-NAVIGATION CONVERSATION CORPUS

The Japanese language, car navigation conversation corpus used in this study was recorded using a Data Collection Vehicle (DCV) system, which supports synchronous recording of multi-modal data including driving signals (e.g., steering angle), driving conditions (e.g., inter-car distance), audio (12 microphones in various places in the car), video (3 different camera angles) and driver biological signals (e.g., heart rate). Subjects were asked to drive along the same 27.7 km driving course (see Fig. 1) while performing several in-car speech tasks. During the navigation conversation task, navigation information was given by one, trained, male navigator through the driver's headphones. Both the subjects and the navigator were native speakers of Japanese.

3. MEASUREMENT TECHNIQUES

3.1. Quality of information transmission during navigation conversations

In this study, we propose our own, novel measurement techniques to assess information transmission quality during navigation conversations, based on the assumption that each driver has a more or less fixed capacity for information processing. When navigation information is difficult to understand, a driver will tend to use more of his or her limited information processing capacity on speech comprehension, which leads to poorer driving performance. Based on this assumption, we can then use differences in a driver's driving performance to measure information transmission quality during navigation conversations. Moreover, to normalize individual differences between drivers , we use the following equation:

$$Q = \frac{P_n - m_n}{V_n}, \tag{1}$$

as our measure of information transmission quality. Here Q stands for information transmission quality, P_n represents the driving performance of driver n, m_n is the average driving performance of driver n on the selected course, and V_n is variance in driving performance during the selected course. To measure driving performance, we use the vehicle's average velocity (mean (V)), the standard deviation of velocity (std. (V)), the standard deviation of acceleration (std. (a)) and the standard deviation of jerk (std. (aa)) during a driving task as our driving performance indicators, based on previous studies of in-car mobile phone conversation [5]. Note that except for mean (V), which has a positive correlation with better driving performance, the other three measures all have a negative correlation with better driving performance.

3.2. Average entropy

In this study, the bi-gram syllabic average entropy of sentence L is calculated using the following equation:

$$H(L) = -\frac{\sum_{t=1}^{T} \log_2 P(w_t|w_{t-1}, G)}{N(s)}. \tag{2}$$

Here T represents the number of morphemes in sentence L, $P(w_t|w_{t-1}, G)$ is the likelihood of the t-th morpheme given language model G, and $N(s)$ is the number of syllables (called "mora" in Japanese) in sentence L. In this study, language model G is appearance frequency of morpheme bigram structures as calculated from web pages, which included about 3 billion morphemes [6].

3.3. Flatness of information transmission rate

As we use a real world conversation corpus for analysis, the information transmission rate changes from time to time. Therefore we propose a simple measurement technique to evaluate the flatness of the information transmission rate of a given speech segment, which can be expressed as:

$$E = -\frac{\sum_{i=1}^{n} |S_i - R| \times d_i}{\sum_{i=1}^{n} d_i}. \tag{3}$$

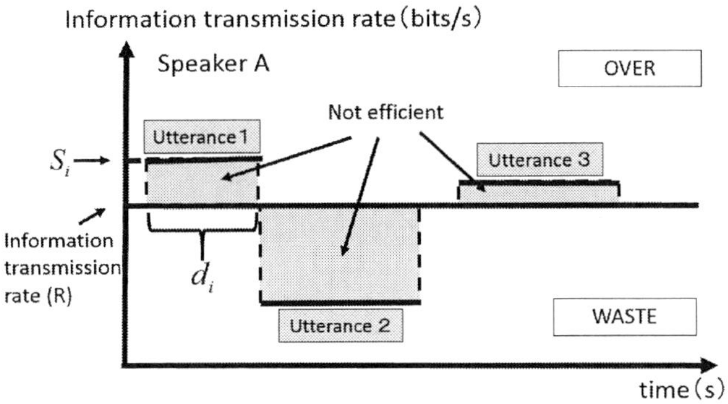

Fig. 2. Conceptual diagram of technique used to measure flatness of information transmission rate.

Here n is the number of sentences in a speech segment, S_i is the information transmission rate of sentence i, R is a fixed information transmission rate, and d_i is the duration of a sentence. Fig. 2 shows the conceptual diagram of our proposed measurement technique. For a given information transmission rate R, we sum up the areas of sentences presented at over rate R and the areas of sentences presented at under rate R (which can be considered as waste if R is a suitable value), and then normalize the sum of each speech segment using its duration. If every sentence in a speech segment is presented at an information transmission rate near R, E converges towards 0.

4. EXPERIMENT

4.1. Experimental set up

As this is a real word driving experiment, the driving environment can have an impact on driving performance (e.g., a traffic jam will result in a lower vehicle velocity). Based on [7], we only select data for which the following two criteria are true: "vehicle in motion" ($V > 6km/h$) and "driving straight ahead" (steering wheel $rotation < 15degrees$), in order to reduce the influence of the driving environment. The subjects were 52 male and 30 female drivers, and each driver drove the course one time. The conversations were transcribed manually with a $2s$ pause to mark the start of a new sentence.

4.2. Relationship between speaking rate and average entropy

Since speaking rate is also an identified characteristic, we normalized the drivers' speaking rate using Eq. (1), substituting speaking rate for driving performance. The relationship between normalized syllabic speaking rate and syllabic average entropy is shown in Fig. 3. Both the drivers' speech and the navigator's speech showed a negative relationship between

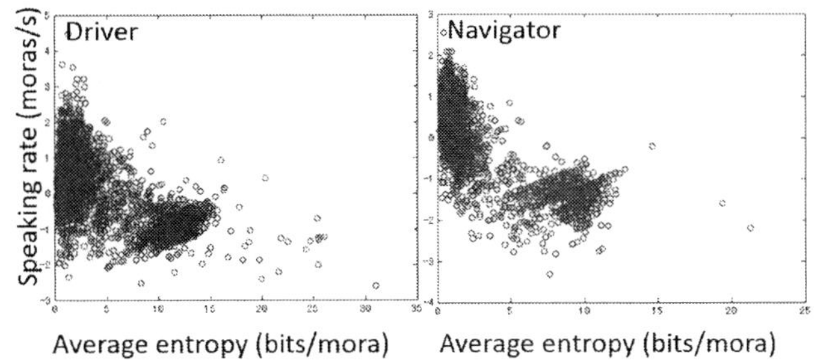

Fig. 3. Relationship between speaking rate and average entropy. Left side represents sentences from drivers' speech (correlation coefficient $= 0.67$), right side represents sentences from navigator's speech (correlation coefficient $= 0.78$).

their normalized syllabic speaking rate and syllabic average entropy. The correlation coefficient between the drivers' speaking rate and average entropy was 0.67 ($sig. < 0.01$), while the correlation coefficient between the navigator's speaking rate and average entropy was 0.78 ($sig. < 0.01$). We can examine this relationship in more detail in Fig. 4, where we calculate the correlation between syllabic speaking rate and average syllabic entropy for each dialog. We can clearly see that the correlation coefficients are negative in most of the segments. This observation supports our hypothesis that we lower our speaking rate when delivering complex messages. The difference in correlation coefficients is probably because we only had one navigator, but had 82 drivers.

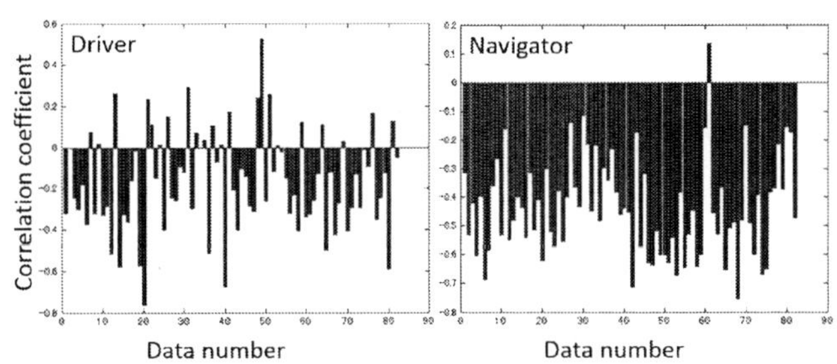

Fig. 4. Correlation between speaking rate and average entropy in every speech segment.

4.3. Effect of flat information transmission rate

Next, we analyze the difference between information transmission quality (driving performance) of navigation instructions given at a flat information transmission rate, and navigation instructions given at varying information transmission rates. In particular, we split the data into two groups using Eq. (3). Group one contains the half of the data that has a larger value in Eq. (3), and group two contains the other half. We then calculate the difference in driving performance between the two groups. As we did not know what was a suitable value for R, we tested the difference between the two groups using different R values. The results are shown in Fig. 5. The group with the flatter navigation information transmission rates exhibited better driving performance when R was larger than $22bits/s$. These results suggest that the flatness of the information transmission rate is correlated with information transmission quality.

In addition, when we split the data from the navigator's speech, the change in inter-group difference shows conformity between different measurement techniques. In contrast, when we split the data from the drivers' speech, which is obviously less correlated with the information transmission quality we want to measure here, the change in inter-group difference shows no conformity. As there is only a weak correlation between our driving performance measurement techniques (about 0.3), perhaps this conformity is due to information transmission quality, and will change in a predictable manner as we change the value of R. According to our observations, $R = 28bits/s$ may be the value of R (i.e., transmission rate) which results in the best information transmission quality for navigation information speech.

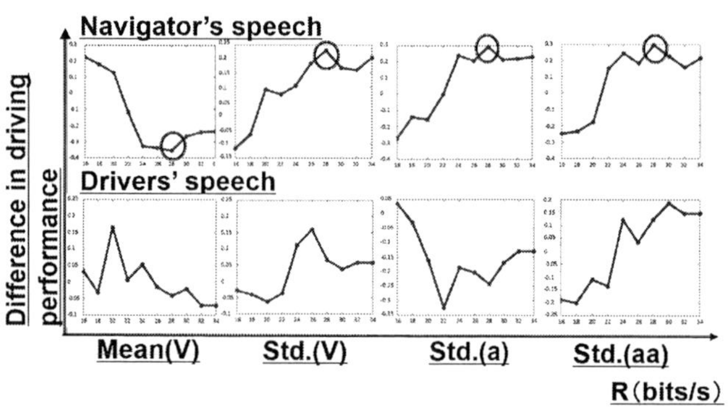

Fig. 5. Difference in driving performance when navigation instructions are presented at flatter and at more variable transmission rates. Average information transmission rate of navigator's speech was $23.8bits/s$, and average information transmission rate of drivers' speech was $21.2bits/s$

5. CONCLUSION

In this study we investigated the relationship between syllabic speaking rate and average syllabic entropy using an in-car navigation dialog corpus. Our results showed that speakers tend to speak more slowly when delivering more complex messages. We also investigated the effect of providing information to drivers at a flatter information transmission rate. Our results suggest that information sent at flatter transmission rates have higher information transmission quality.

Although we only used "vehicle in motion" and "driving straight ahead" data, the environmental situation could still have had a significant impact on driving performance. Therefore, we cannot definitively conclude that differences in driving performance in this study were caused by differences in information transmission rates. Nevertheless, as there was only one navigator, it is unlikely that there is any difference in the flatness of the information transmission rate between the two groups we analyzed (although they are different statistically). However, the corpus used in our experiment lacked strong control of the driving environment, therefore in order to confirm that differences in driving performance are actually the result of variation in the navigator's speaking rate, we need to reduce the possible impact of the driving environment.

6. ACKNOWLEDGEMENT

This research is supported by the Center of Innovation Program (Nagoya-COI; Mobility Society leading to an Active and Joyful Life for Elderly) from Japan Science and Technology Agency.

7. REFERENCES

[1] G. K. Zipf, "The psycho-biology of language." *1935*

[2] B. Sigurd, M. Eeg - Olofsson, and Van Weijer,. "Word length, sentence length and frequency?Zipf revisited." *Studia Linguistica, 2004, 58.1: 37-52.*

[3] S. T. Piantadosi, H. Tily, and E. Gibson, "Word lengths are optimized for efficient communication." *Proceedings of the National Academy of Sciences, 2011, 108.9: 3526-3529.*

[4] T. F. Jaeger, "Redundancy and reduction: Speakers manage syntactic information density." *Cognitive psychology, 2010, 61.1: 23-62.*

[5] W. J. Horrey, and C. D. Wickens, "Examining the impact of cell phone conversations on driving using meta-analytic techniques." *Human Factors: The Journal of the Human Factors and Ergonomics Society, 2006, 48.1: 196-205.*

[6] http://plata.ar.media.kyotou.ac.jp/gologo/lm.html

[7] N. Kawaguchi, S. Matsubara, K. Takeda, and F. Itakura, "CIAIR In-Car Speech Corpus–Influence of Driving Status–." *IEICE transactions on information and systems, 2005, 88.3: 578-582.*

Driving Scene Classification Using Vehicle Motion Estimated with Smartphone

Masayuki Tsuboi[1], Chiyomi Miyajima[1], and Kazuya Takeda[2]

[1] Graduate School of Information Science, Nagoya University, Japan
[2] Institute of Innovation for Future Society, Nagoya University, Japan
E-mail: {tsuboi.masayuki, miyajima, takeda}@g.sp.m.is.nagoya-u.ac.jp

Abstract We investigate a driving scene classification method using driving data obtained from the sensors embedded in smartphones such as an accelerometer, GPS, and a camera. Right and left turns, stops, right and left lane changes, and cruising are modeled with hidden Markov models using vehicle acceleration, vehicle velocity estimated with GPS, and optical flows calculated from video images of the road ahead. A driving scene classification experiment is conducted using driving data recorded on city streets and an expressway. We found that histograms of optical flow vectors in four directions effectively represented vehicle motion, achieving classification with F-values of about 0.7, outperforming the combined use of vehicle acceleration and velocity information.

Keywords Driving scene classification, optical flow, hidden Markov model, smartphone

1 INTRODUCTION

Some advanced driver assistance system studies use sensor-rich instrumented vehicles equipped with expensive sensors, such as omni-directional cameras and distance sensors, etc. [1], to recognize various driving situations. Such sensors can be expensive and difficult to mount in subjects' personal vehicles, so methods of recognizing driving scenes using low-cost and easy-to-mount sensors are also needed.

In this paper we investigate a driving scene classification method using the sensors embedded in smartphones. Since smartphone accelerometers and GPS may not be sufficiently accurate to precisely measure vehicle acceleration and velocity, we also use optical flows [2] calculated from video images of the road ahead, recorded with the smartphone's camera. Histogram of optical flow vectors in four directions (right, left, up, and down) is used to represent vehicle motion.

Driving scenes of right and left turns, stops, right and left lane changes, and cruising are modeled with hidden Markov models using acceleration and velocity data, as well as histograms of optical flow vectors. In order to evaluate our classification method, we conduct driving scene classification experiments using driving data recorded on city streets and an expressway

2 ESTIMATION OF VEHICLE MOTION

Vehicle motion can be estimated from vehicle acceleration and velocity. However, vehicle acceleration measured with the accelerometer embedded in a smartphone, and vehicle velocity calculated using smartphone GPS locations may not be accurate enough to measure vehicle motion. For this reason, we also estimate vehicle motion using video images recorded with a smartphone camera.

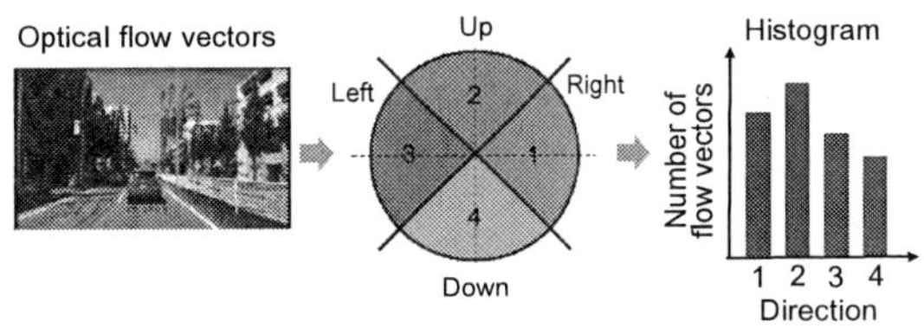

Fig. 1. Histogram of optical flow vectors

We focus on optical flow vectors in four directions (right, left, up, and down), as shown in Fig. 1. Histograms of these optical flow vectors in four directions are then used as features for modeling driving situations.

3 EXPERIMENT

3.1 Recording Driving Data

We mounted a smartphone (Galaxy Nexus GT-I9250M) on the interior of vehicle windshields, behind the rear-view mirrors. Acceleration, GPS location, and frontal video images were then recorded by the sensors embedded in the smartphone. Driving data was recorded as each of three drivers drove a distance of about 5 km on city streets around Nagoya University, and as they drove a distance of about 20 km on the Tokyo-Nagoya expressway (Fig. 2).

We then classified the driving scenes into one of the six following categories:

- Right turn
- Left turn
- Right lane change
- Left lane change
- Stop
- Cruising (all other driving)

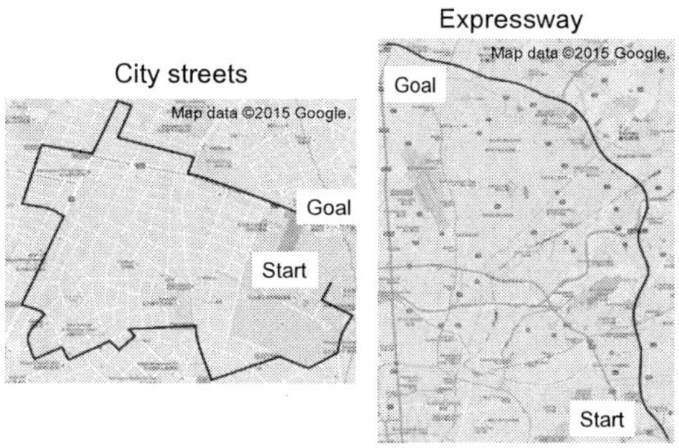

Fig. 2. Driving routes on city streets and expressway

To obtain the ground truth of each driving situation, driving data was manually annotated and classified into one of the above mentioned categories. Driving data recorded on city streets was classified into only four categories (right turn, left turn, stop, and cruising) because there were few lane change scenes. On the other hand, driving data recorded on the expressway was classified into three categories (right lane change, left lane change, and cruising) because there were no intersections on the expressway, so the drivers never turned to the right or left and never stopped.

3.2 Experimental Conditions

Each driving scene was modeled with left-to-right hidden Markov models (HMMs) using longitudinal and lateral acceleration data, GPS-based velocity, and/or a histogram of the optical flow vectors. A driving scene classification experiment was then conducted to evaluate the effectiveness of the method using histograms of the optical flow vectors by cross-validation. F-values were used to compare classification performance.

3.3 Results

Figure 3 shows the results of our driving scene classification experiment. We can see that the histogram of the optical flow vectors outperformed a combination of acceleration and velocity data, achieving F-values of about 0.7.

Tables 1 and 2 show the detailed F-value results for city streets and expressway driving, respectively. In both situations, cruising and stopping were more accurately classified than turning and lane changes, both of which are associated with lateral movement to the right or left. Classification performance was especially low for right turns. This might be because there is wider variation in right turn situations in Japan, e.g., drivers need to slow down and yield to oncoming vehicles and to pedestrians at crosswalks. Lane change detection accuracy could be further improved by detecting the lane markers using the video images.

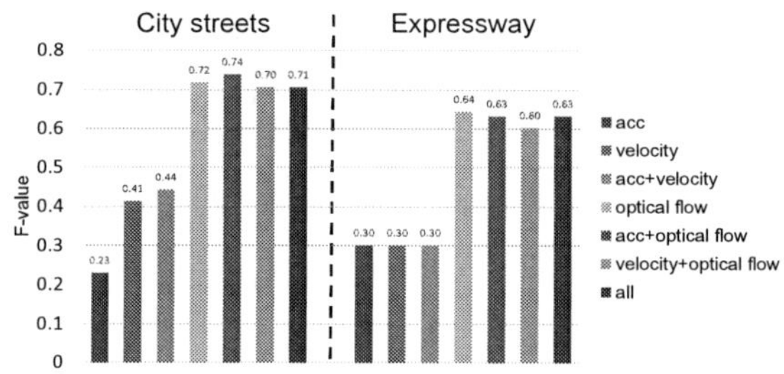

Fig. 3. Results of driving scene classification experiment

Table 1. F-values for city street scenes

Cruising	Stop	Right turn	Left turn
0.89	0.92	0.42	0.71

Table 2. F-values for expressway scenes

Cruising	Right lane change	Left lane change
0.87	0.40	0.65

4 CONCLUSION

We investigated a driving scene classification method which estimated vehicle motion using driving data obtained from a smartphone. A driving scene classification experiment was then conducted using driving data recorded on city streets and an expressway. We found that a method using histograms of optical flow vectors in four directions achieved F-values of about 0.7, outperforming a method using a combination of vehicle acceleration and velocity data.

Classification performance could be further improved through the use of additional information obtained from vehicles' CAN-bus and through the detection of surrounding vehicles and lane markers.

Acknowledgment

This work was partially supported by a Grant-in-Aid for Scientific Research (C), No.15K002231, from the Japan Society for the Promotion of Science (JSPS).

5 REFERENCES

[1] K. Takeda, J. Hansen, P. Boyraz, L. Malta, C. Miyajima, and H. Abut, "International large-scale vehicle corpora for research on driver behavior on the road," IEEE Transactions on Intelligent Transportation Systems, Vol. 12, No. 4, pp. 1609-1623, Dec. 2011.

[2] R. Chaudhry, A. Ravichandran, G. Hager, and R. Vidal, "Histograms of oriented optical flow and Binet-Cauchy kernels on nonlinear dynamical systems for the recognition of human actions," IEEE Conference on Computer Vision and Pattern Recognition, pp. 1932-1939, June 2009.

Risky Lane Change Detection Based on Symbolization of Driving Data

Suguru Yamazaki[1], Chiyomi Miyajima[1], Masataka Mori[2], Takashi Bando[3], Kazuhito Takenaka[2], and Kazuya Takeda[4]

[1]: Graduate School of Information Science, Nagoya University, Nagoya, Japan
[2]: Corporate R&D Div. 3, DENSO CORPORATION, Kariya, Aichi, Japan
[3]: NA Research Laboratory, DENSO INTERNATIONAL AMERICA, INC., San Jose, CA, USA
[4]: Institute of Innovation for Future Society, Nagoya University, Nagoya, Japan
E-mail: yamazaki.suguru@g.sp.m.is.nagoya-u.ac.jp

Abstract We propose a method of detecting risky lane changes within large-scale driving corpora, employing a hierarchical symbolization approach consisting of a nonparametric extension of hidden Markov model and a statistical language model for data-driven symbolization of driving data. We use vehicle velocity, force on gas and brake pedals, steering wheel angle, and their dynamics of these forces for the symbolization of driving data. Latent Dirichlet allocation (LDA) is then applied to associate the symbols with driving behavior. Each symbol can be represented as topic proportions estimated by the LDA. We detect risky lane changes based on the topic proportions. We also investigate the effectiveness of using data about the surrounding driving environment. By using both vehicle operation and surrounding environment information, we are able to achieve better risky lane change detection performance than when using either type of data alone.

Keywords Large-scale driving data, symbolization, risky lane change, hidden Markov model, unsupervised morphological analysis

1. INTRODUCTION

The number of deaths from traffic accidents has been reduced in recent years due to advanced driver assistance systems (ADASs). However, according to the National HighWay Traffic Safety Administration (NHTSA), 32,675 Americans died in traffic accidents in 2014 [1]. Therefore, more must be done to improve driving safety.

Since newer vehicles are equipped with various sensors, we can easily collect driving data on vehicle motion, driver behavior, and the surrounding environment. There are some active research projects which use large amounts of driving data to effectively investigate safety issues. For example, the SHRP2 project [2] has collected continuous driving data from 3,200 of drivers, and the EuroFOT project [3] has evaluated ADASs for more than 1,000 drivers. Although large-scale driving corpora have been collected as a result of such projects, it is difficult to utilize the driving data effectively for further research due to their size and heterogeneity.

Taniguchi et al. [4] proposed an unsupervised method for segmenting driving behavior data into semiotic symbols, known as Double Articulation Analyzer (DAA), which can be used to represent driving situations observed within driving data corpora. By combining this symbolization of driving data with latent Dirichlet allocation (LDA), Bando et al. [5] translated these symbols into "driving behavior topics" in natural language. Mori et al. [6] also achieved good performance when extracting specific driving behavior from driving data corpora. DAA is an efficient method for segmenting driving-situations when dealing with large amounts of driving data.

In this paper, we propose a method of using symbolized driving corpora data to understand driving behavior. We employ DAA to segment and symbolize driving behavior data, and LDA to associate the symbols with detailed behavioral and environmental information. A polynomial linear regression model is trained to predict the degree of risk in driving scenes using topic proportions estimated by LDA. To evaluate the effectiveness of this symbolization framework, we conduct a risky lane change detection experiment and compare detection performance when using both driving behavior data and information about the surrounding environment with performance when using either type of data alone.

2. SYMBOLIZATION FRAMEWORK

2.1. Symbolization of Large-Scale Driving Corpus

An overview of the driving data symbolization algorithm is shown in Fig 1. Sequences of vehicle operation data are represented as sequences of meaningful units called "chunks" using DAA. DAA as proposed by Taniguchi et al. [4] is a hierarchical symbolization approach, consisting of a sticky hierarchical Dirichlet process hidden Markov model (sHDP-HMM) [7] and a nested Pitman-Yor language model (NPYLM) [8]. In the first step, driving behavior data is converted into a sequence of segments which describe short-term vehicle operation, using sHDP-HMM. Then, NPYLM is used to divide the sequence of segments into chunks according to their emergence frequencies, which correspond to long-term

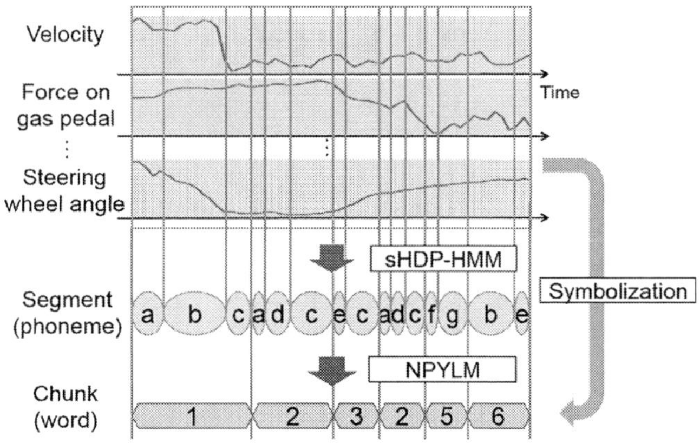

Fig. 1. Overview of symbolization algorithm

driving behavior. These chunks are expected to describe a meaningful driving context. Although the numbers of segments and chunks, which correspond to phonemes and words in natural language, are actually unknown, they can be automatically determined from the driving behavior data set using the unsupervised method.

2.2. Interpretation of Driving Situation in Symbols

Due to the unsupervised method used to symbolize the data, it is difficult to understand driving contexts from the sequences of symbols. To deal with the problem, Bando et al. [5] applied LDA to sequences of chunks and associated them with driving behavior information. LDA [9] is widely used for natural language processing as a generative model for documents with multiple topics (e.g., sports, politics, economics) where words related to each topic are distributed within the entire document. Using LDA, each document can be represented or characterized as a set of topic proportions, which are determined by how often certain words appear in the document. In order to represent driving behavior which corresponds to each chunk as topic proportions, Bando et al. [5] used the histogram of the raw sensor data included in each chunk as a document and each bin of the histogram corresponded to a word in the document. Figure 2 shows an overview of the LDA approach. This approach allows us to successfully extract intuitive characteristics of driving behavior from each chunk.

3. DETECTION OF RISKY LANE CHANGES

We now attempt to detect risky lane changes within a symbolized driving corpus. We also evaluate the effectiveness of using information about the surrounding environment in LDA.

3.1. Driving Corpus

In this study, we used expressway driving data from NUDrive corpus [10].

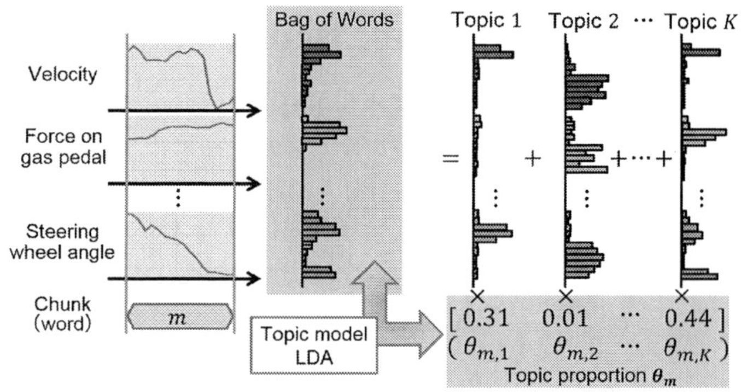

Fig. 2. Overview of LDA approach

Table 1. Driving data set

Amount of data	8.45 hours
Number of subjects	11
Recorded signals	Force on gas/brake pedals, Steering wheel angle, Vehicle velocity and Δ of the above 4 features
Sampling rate	10 Hz

Table 2. Result of chunking

Number of chunks	7046
Number of unique chunks	882
Mean length of chunks	4.161 sec

Table 1 shows the driving data used for symbolization and Table 2 shows the result of applying DAA to the driving data.

The data set includes 496 lane changes to the right and 492 to the left. The degree of risk involved in each lane change was rated by subjective evaluation. Ten Subjects watched video of the lane change scenes, viewing the area in front of the vehicle, and rated how risky they felt the driver's behavior was in each scene, from 1 (safest) to 5 (riskiest). We regrarded the mean value of the ten subjects' evaluations as the ground truth degree of risk. We defined lane changes whose degrees of risk were in the top 5 percent as risky lane changes.

3.2. Surrounding Environment Information

In general, driving behavior is affected by vehicle motion, driver behavior, and surrounding environment. The surrouding environment, in particular, may have a great influence on lane change behavior. Therefore, we employed time headway (THW) to the surrounding vehicles to represent the driving environment. THW is a difference between the time when a vehicle arrives at a location and the time when the next vehicle arrives at the same point, which can be represented as

$$t_{\mathrm{H}} = \frac{|\Delta D|}{v_{\mathrm{host}}}, \tag{1}$$

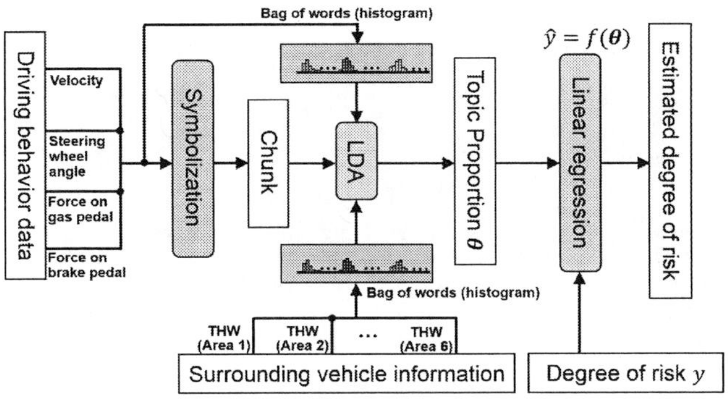

Fig. 3. Overview of estimating the degrees of risk for lane changes

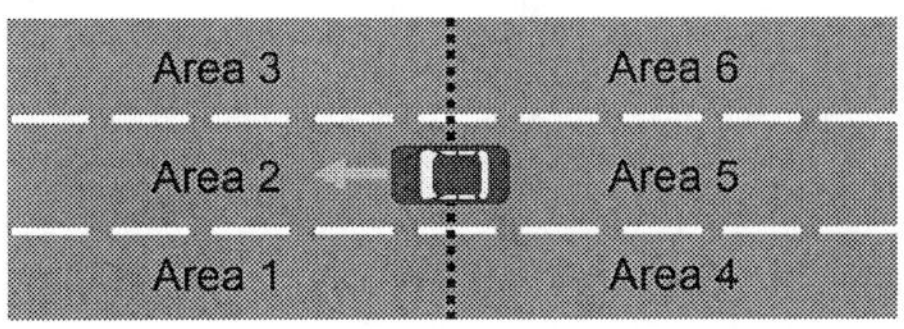

Fig. 4. Six areas surrounding a driver's vehicle

where ΔD is the relative distance, and where v_{host} is the velocity of the driver's vehicle. We divided the area around the driver's own vehicle into six areas as shown in Fig. 4. We applied LDA [9] to the surrounding environment information by assuming the histogram of the THW of each chunk was a document and each bin of the histogram was a word.

3.3. Estimation of Degree of Risk Using Topic Proportions

To detect risly lane changes, we used the following linear regression model:

$$\hat{y} = f(\boldsymbol{\theta}) = \sum_{n=1}^{N} \sum_{k=1}^{K} a_{n,k}(\theta_k)^n, \tag{2}$$

where $\hat{y}$ is the estimated degree of risk, $\boldsymbol{\theta}$ is the topic proportion and K is the number of topics. Our goal is to determine function f in (2).

Figure 3 shows an overview of the procedure for estimating the degree of risk involved in lane changes contained in a driving data corpus. The procedure can be summarized as follows:

a) Divide raw driving behavior data into sequences of segments and chunks using DAA [4]
b) Estimate topic proportions with LDA [5] using both raw driving behavior data and/or information about the surrounding environment
c) Estimate the degree of risk using linear regression using the topic proportions

Table 3. AUCs under different conditions.

# of topics	Right lane change			Left lane change		
	I	II	III	I	II	III
20	0.791	0.823	0.839	0.829	0.758	0.770
25	0.783	0.842	0.834	0.823	0.798	0.830
30	0.826	0.837	0.867	0.817	0.8054	0.856
35	0.778	0.825	0.862	0.810	0.833	0.866
40	0.806	0.847	0.848	0.807	0.841	0.849
50	0.804	0.849	0.851	0.804	0.799	0.847

4. EXPERIMENT

4.1. Experimental Conditions

We used the proposed method to detect risky lane changes in the previously described NUDrive expressway corpus data. The number of topics K was set to 20, 25, 30, 35, 40, and 50. Furthermore, in order to confirm the advantage of using data representing the surrounding enviroment for LDA, we compared detection performance under the following conditions:

I. Using only driving behavior data (velocity, force on pedals, steering wheel angle, and the dynamic features of these variables) for LDA
II. Using only surrouding environment information (THWs) for LDA
III. Using both behavioral data and surrouding environment information for LDA

We evaluated detection performance using leave-one-out cross validation. We employed area under ROC curves (AUCs) as the measure of detection performance.

4.2. Result

Table 3 shows risky lane change detection performance results under the various conditions described above. For example, the optimal number of topics under condition III was 30 for right lane changes and 35 for left changes. We achieved better detection performance when we used both driving behavior data and surrounding environment information.

Figure 5 shows the histograms of the intensity of behavior data and THW for each topic under condition III as trained using LDA. We can see that there were topics which included both behavior data and THW features (e.g., topic 27, topic 29).

Figure 6 shows the histograms of THWs during left lane changes whose degrees of the risk were in the top and bottom 5 percent. The vertical axis represents bin numbers of THWs represented as 20 discrete values. For the values of THW t_{H} less than 3.0 [sec], we allocated the value from bin 1 to bin 19, otherwise the values were assigned to bin 20. To sum up, the lower the bin number, the riskier the lane change. We found that THWs in areas 1, 3, and 5 had a marked impact on the degree of risk, because most of THWs were assigned to bin 20

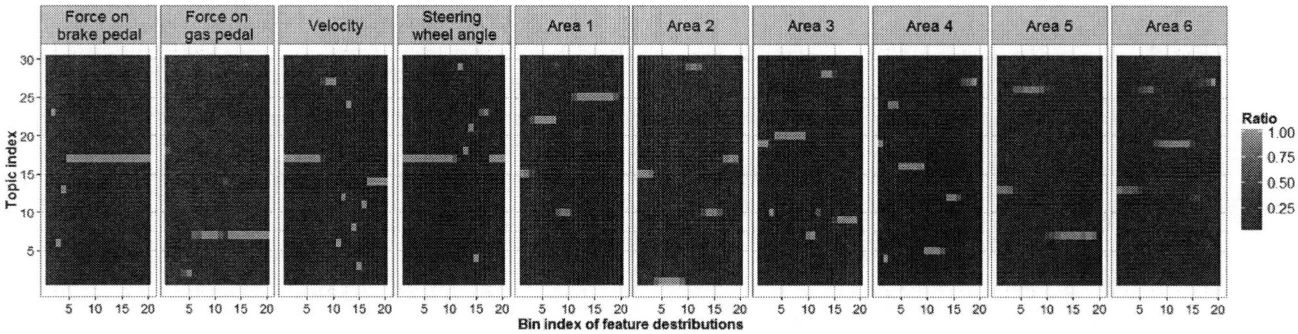

Fig. 5. Histograms of intensity of behavior data and THWs in each topic under condition III

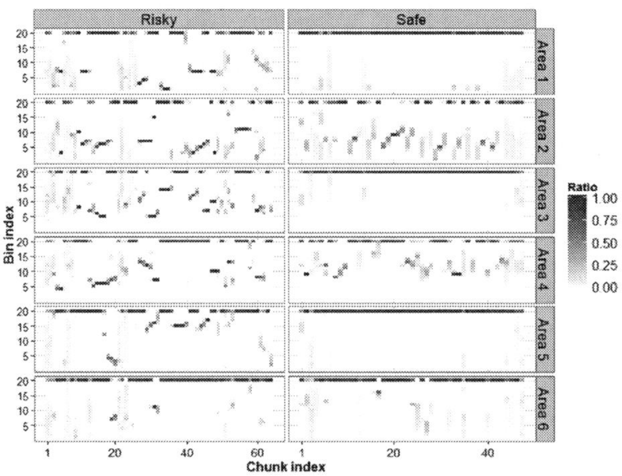

Fig. 6. Histograms of THW during left lane changes whose degrees of risk were in the top or bottom 5 %

in safe lane changes, while more THWs distributed between bins 1-19 in risky lane changes.

5. CONCLUSIONS

In this paper, we proposed a method for detecting risky lane changes based on symbolization of driving data. We first applied DAA to segment the driving behavior data, and then LDA to describe driving behavior in each chunk. Polynomial linear regression was used to predict the degree of risk from topic proportions obtained with LDA. As a result, when using both vehicle motion and surrounding environment information for LDA, we obtained better risky lane change detection performance than when using either type of information alone. We found that a symbolizarion framework could be used effectively with surrounding environment information.

Our future work includes evaluation of the effectiveness of applying DAA to surrounding environment information.

Acknowledgment

This work was partially supported by a Grant-in-Aid for Scientific Research (C) under No.15K002231, from the Japan Society for the Promotion of Science (JSPS).

6. REFERENCES

[1] NHTSA: Early Estimate of Motor Vehicle Traffic Fatalities in 2014, June 2015.

[2] A. Blatt, J. Pierowicz, M. Flanigan, P.-S. Lin, A. Kourtellis, P. Jovanis, J. Jenness, M. Wilaby, J. Campbell, C. Richard, D. Good, N. Czar, and M. Hoover, "Naturalistic Driving Study: Field Data Collection," *Technical report, Transportation Research Board of the National Academies*, 2014.

[3] M. Benmimoun, A. Putz, A. Zlocki, and L. Eckstein, "euro-FOT: Field Operatinal Test and Impact Assessment of Advanced Driver Assistance Systems: Final Results," *FISITA World Automotive Congress*, pp. 537–547, 2012.

[4] T. Taniguchi, S. Nagasaka, K. Hitomi, N. Chandrasiri, and T. Bando, "Semiotic Prediction of Driving Behavior using Unsupervised Double Articulation Analyzer," *Proc. IEEE IV*, pp. 849–854, 2012.

[5] T. Bando, K. Takenaka, S. Nagasaka, and T. Taniguchi, "Generating Contextual Description from Driving Behavioral Data," *Proc. IEEE IV*, pp. 183–189, 2014.

[6] M. Mori, K. Takenaka, T. Bando, T. Taniguchi, C. Miyajima, and K. Takeda, "Automatic Lane Change Extraction based on Temporal Patterns of Symbolized Driving Behavioral Data," *Proc. IEEE IV*, pp. 976–981, 2015.

[7] E. B. Fox, E. B. Sudderth, M. I. Jordan, and A. S. Willsky, "The sticky HDP-HMM: Bayesian Nonparametric Hidden Markov Models with Persistent States," MIT Laboratory for Information and Decision Systems, Tech. Rep. 2777, 2007.

[8] D. Mochihashi, T. Yamada, and N. Ueda, "Bayesian Unsupervised Word Segmentation with Nested Pitman-Yor Language Modeling," *Proc. ACL and AFNLP*, vol. 1, pp.100–108, 2009.

[9] D. M. Blei, A. Y. Ng, and M. I. Jordan, "Latent Dirichlet Allocation," *Journal of Machine Learning Research*, vol. 3, pp. 993–1022, 2003.

[10] K. Takeda, J. H. Hansen, P. Boyraz, L. Malta, C. Miyajima, and H. Abut, "International Large-Scale Vehicle Corpora for Research on Driver Behavior on the Road," *IEEE Transactions on Intelligent Transportation Systems*, vol. 12, no. 4, pp. 1609–1623, 2011.

Driver Performance Level Estimation Method Using Driver-Vehicle Dynamics Data Based on Control-Oriented Driver Models

Pongsathorn Raksincharoensak[1], Shintaro Saigo[1] and Masao Nagai[2]

[1]: Tokyo University of Agriculture and Technology, Japan
[2]: Japan Automobile Research Institute, Japan
E-mail: pong@cc.tuat.ac.jp

Abstract

This paper presents the theoretical model-based methodology to identify the driver performance level from the driver-vehicle behavior without using direct measurement of physiological data. Knowing driver performance level during driving can potentially avoid severe accidents which might occur due to driver performance degradation, e.g. drowsiness. It was reported that highway fatalities in Japan have been increasing over the past 3 years although traffic fatalities have been decreasing. Most of accidents on highway are caused by careless driving as well as drowsiness. Therefore, a number of researches on driving drowsiness detection have been carried out, and various detection methods have been proposed. Examples of the methods using physiological data include percent of eye lid closure, heart rate, electroencephalogram (EEG), facial expression, etc. These direct measurement methods need extra sensors which would be a problem with the implementation cost and difference among individual drivers becomes an issue of the detection system parameter optimization. On the other hand, measurement of driver-vehicle behavior data can be used to infer the driver state by monitoring driver performance level from his/her driving operation with respect to the road environment input. This approach does not need any directly intrusive measurement on the drivers, so the estimation can be done with existing on-board vehicle sensors. Here, it is important to find the correlation between the actual driver state and the driver-vehicle behavior data as well as to clarify the features which can precisely identify the driver performance level as well as detect low driving performance, e.g. driving drowsiness.

Therefore, this paper investigates the objective measures for the drowsiness level using the estimated driver performance level based on the reference control-oriented driver models. The major findings from the study can be used for the individual adaptation of advanced driver assistance systems, for instance changing the timing of the warning system or the intensity of the control intervention, which can potentially improve driver acceptance as well as enhance the accident avoidance performance of the system.

The key point of the estimation algorithm proposed in this study is to infer the driver performance level from the deviation from the normal-state driver model, which refers to his/her naturalistic driving behavior. Using this methodology, the driver state can be potentially identified based on the individual driver characteristics, so that appropriate assistance maneuvers by advanced driver assistance systems can be provided timely and adapted to various types of drivers.

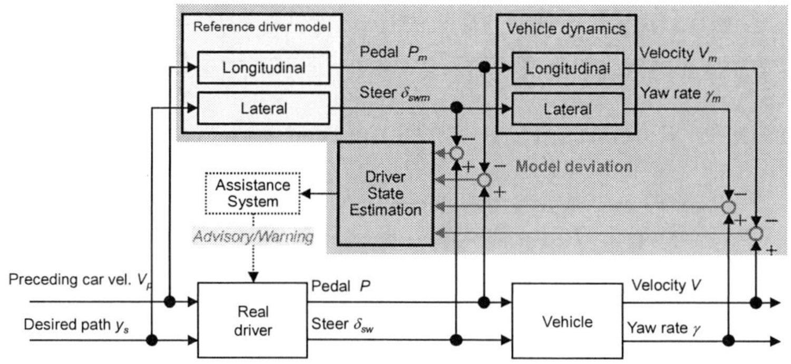

Fig.1 Model-based driver performance level estimation

Fig. 1 shows the conceptual diagram of a model-based method of estimating driver performance level. In the estimation part of this study, the reference driver models for car-following and lane-keeping maneuvers are embedded and the desired vehicle dynamics output can be calculated. The parameters in these models were identified by using the driving data collected in similar driving situation. Comparing the output variables from the reference driver model with the actual measured driving data, the driving performance level can be quantitatively estimated from the degree of deviation.

The deviation of each variable with respect to the model-based calculated value is calculated at each sampling time. The variance of the model deviation with respect to the reference driver model during a certain time interval, 30 seconds, is used to identify the driver performance level. Fig.2 shows the correlation of the variance of the gas pedal, steering wheel angle, velocity and yaw rate deviation with respect to the driver drowsiness level (1 = normal, awake, 5 = strongly sleepy). The correlation between the variance of the model deviation and the driver performance level degradation was found from the experiment study.

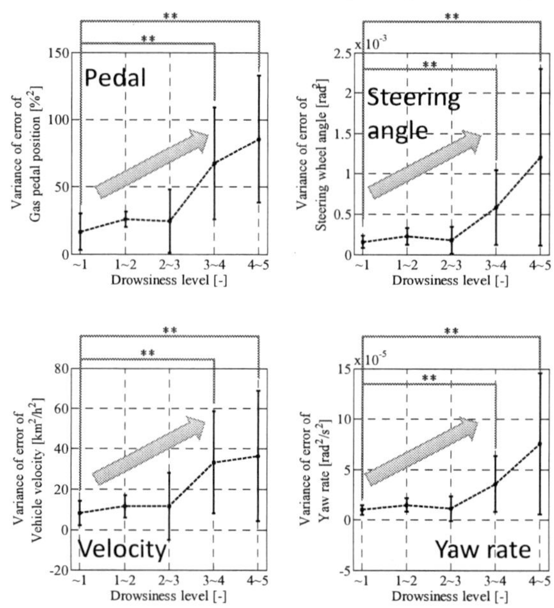

Fig.2 Correlation between driver drowsiness and objective driver-vehicle behavior data

Keywords

Driver assistance, Active safety, Driver Monitoring, Driver Performance Level, Driver Model

Spectral Distance Analysis for Quality Estimation of In-Car Communication Systems

Anne Theiß[1], Gerhard Schmidt[1]

[1]: Digital Signal Processing and System Theory, Christian-Albrechts-Universität zu Kiel
E-mail: ath/gus@tf.uni-kiel.de

Abstract The communication inside a vehicle can be impaired by a high background noise while driving at medium or higher velocities and by the unusual orientation of the passengers as they are not facing each other. As a consequence the passengers often start to raise their voices and to change their positions by leaning forward or, in case of the front passengers, turning backwards to improve this situation. These adaptations to the communication situation may be uncomfortable, exhausting, and might result in a security risk if the driver turns around. An in-car communication system (ICC system) can improve the communication by recording the speech signals and reproducing the enhanced signals over the loudspeakers inside the compartment that are close to the listening passengers.

After and during the design and development of such systems, the achieved quality is of great interest. Therefore, a spectral distance approach is presented in this contribution. Even if spectral distance measures are well established and often used for quality evaluation in speech communication systems, we face here a special challenge, which is the creation of an appropriate reference signal. In addition, an investigation of the reliability of the proposed quality estimate by means of a subjective listening test was performed and the results are presented.

Keywords In-Car Communication Systems, Evaluation, Spectral Distance

1. INTRODUCTION

The communication inside a vehicle can be impaired due to a high background noise occurring especially at higher velocities. In addition, the speech signal is attenuated by the orientation of the passengers, since they are facing the windshield and not each other. Therefore, the signal-to-noise ratio (SNR) at the ears of the listening passenger, for example sitting on one of the rear seats, is decreased. In order to improve this impaired communication situation, the passengers start to modify their vocal effort which results mainly in a higher speech level. This is referred as the so-called Lombard effect [1]. In addition, they are leaning towards each other in order to reduce the distance respectively change their orientation. All these modifications can be exhausting for the passengers and can affect the safety of the passengers if the driver turns around.

Technical solutions to enhance the communication in vehicles are so-called In-Car Communication systems (ICC systems) [2, 3, 4]. Such systems record the speech signal of the talking passenger by means of the installed microphones, and plays back the enhanced speech signal via those loudspeakers positioned close to the listening passenger.

After and during the development of ICC systems, their quality is of great interest. In order to evaluate an ICC system, reproducible and instrumental measures which predict the subjective quality evaluation are needed. Even if this research is rather new, several authors already published some work in this field [5, 6, 7]. In this contribution, an evaluation method based on a spectral distance is proposed. A common spectral distance approach compares the original speech signal with the processed signal. But, however, for a human being the desired speech signal in this environment might be something different. The listening passenger can be disturbed, when perceiving two versions of one sound event. Which event is desired and which is disturbing is highly depending on the power ratio and the delay between both events. Hence, the choice of the reference is not trivial.

In the upcoming sections this problem will be addressed and a solution will be proposed. After deriving an appropriate reference, the spectral distance which is developed for estimating the quality of an ICC system is defined. As a last step the results of the proposed measure is compared to the results of a subjective listening test.

2. SYSTEM DESCRIPTION

In Fig. 1, a sedan equipped with a basic ICC system supporting only the direction from front to rear, with only one microphone and one loudspeaker, is depicted. This system does not correspond to a typical ICC system implementation, which usual utilizes more than one microphone and loudspeaker. But it eases the derivation of the measure proposed within this contribution. The resulting measure is of course applicable to other more complex ICC systems.

In order to create a reproducible evaluation setup, a realistic driving noise simulation which can be calibrated to reproduce always the same noise impression is utilized, see [8]. In Fig. 1, the driver seat is occupied by an artificial talking passenger (mouth loudspeaker reproducing the test signal) and the rear seat behind the driver by an artificial listening pas-

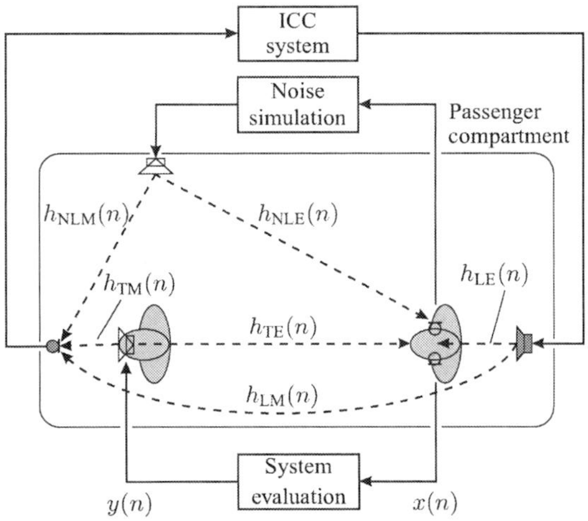

Fig. 1. Basic structure of the ICC system evaluation [7].

senger (two ear microphones). These two artificial passengers represent the input and the output of the evaluation module.

The spectral distance is derived by means of the ear signal $x(n)$ and a modified version of the test signal $y(n)$, in the following called reference signal. As mentioned before, the derivation of the reference signal is depending on the delay and the power of the transmission. Therefore, a delay and a frequency-dependent gain alignment has to be performed. Deriving these adjustments of the test signal in a reliable way is a crucial task when developing the proposed measure.

3. SPECTRAL DISTANCE MEASURE

The conversation participants inside a vehicle equipped with an ICC system perceive two versions of the desired speech signal:

- One is the direct sound, coming from the talking passenger, which has usually a rather low level.
- The second version is produced by the ICC system via the loudspeakers inside the vehicle. This second speech signal can increase the reverberation inside the vehicle, but also increases the speech level at the ear of the listening passenger and hence, improves the communication situation. This second sound event has, depending on the scenario and therefore on the adjustment of the ICC system, a higher level than the direct sound.

Out of these superposed sound events a reasonable reference signal needs to be estimated. In a first step the two signals, the ear signal $x(n)$ and the mouth signal $y(n)$, are aligned in time, see Fig. 2. The gain of these two signals is aligned in a second step.

3.1. Delay Alignment

The delay is estimated by means of a cross-correlation analysis between the mouth and the ear $x(n)$, where the mouth signal corresponds to the test signal $y(n)$ from Fig. 3. Both signals are first passed through a high-pass filter with cut-off frequency 100 Hz and the delay is derived by

$$\delta = \arg\max_{\kappa}\Big\{ \mathrm{E}\left\{\breve{x}(n)\breve{y}(n+\kappa)\right\} \Big\}, \tag{1}$$

where $\breve{x}(n)$ and $\breve{y}(n)$ correspond to the high-pass filtered mouth and ear signals. Due to this cross-correlation analysis the delay between the artificial mouth and the signal with the highest amplitude reaching the ear microphone is estimated. Meaning, if the speech signal transmitted by the ICC system has a higher level than the direct component, the delay between the ICC signal and the mouth signal will be estimated. In the opposite case, the delay of the direct component is estimated and utilized for the evaluation.

3.2. Gain Alignment

The evaluation is realized within a real-time framework in the frequency domain in order to create a sequential and frequency-depending spectral distance, see Fig. 2. Therefore,

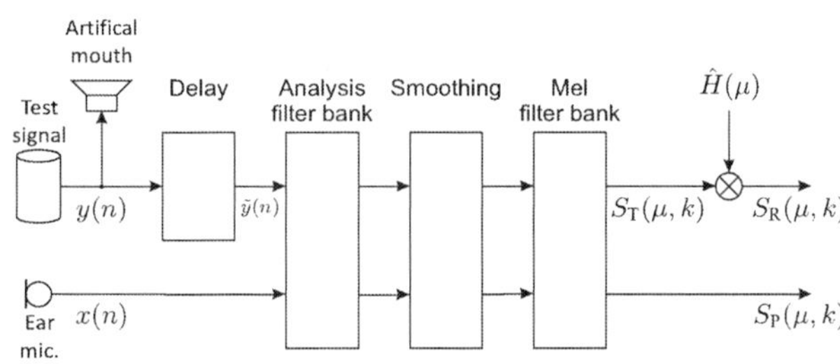

Fig. 2. Signal processing of spectral distance analysis within a real-time framework.

an analysis filter bank using a Hann window $w(n)$ with a length of N_{FFT} samples is applied. The complex spectrum of $x(n)$ is given by $X(\mu,k)$ where k corresponds to the frame index and μ to the frequency bin. Subsequently, the magnitude spectra are smoothed in ascending and descending frequency direction by a zero-phase, first-order infinite impulse response filter. A Mel filter bank, see Fig. 2, is applied to take the human perception of sounds into account.

In order to determine the gain alignment $\hat{H}(\mu)$, a test signal $y(n)$ containing speech passages and short noise passages is utilized. The speech passages as well as the noise simulation mentioned before (see Fig. 1) are necessary to transfer the ICC system into the desired operational state. Since an ICC system can react sensitively against noise excitations, these passages are set to a duration of about 100 ms and, in addition, are exciting only a selected frequency range.

During these noise passages the power spectral density (PSD) of the test signal and the processed signals is estimated.

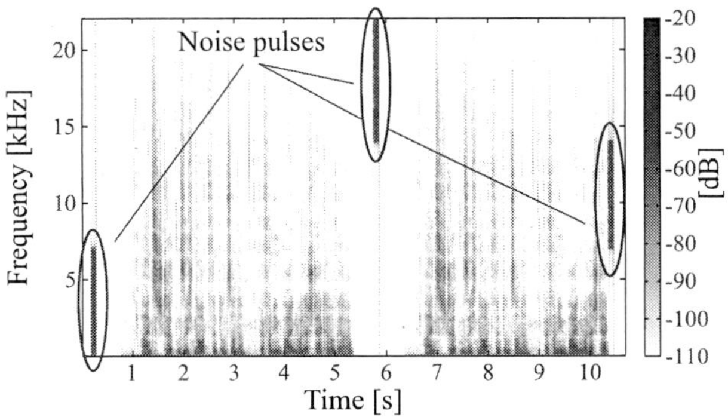

Fig. 3. Example of a test signal used for estimating the gain alignment.

The PSD in dB of the reference signal is

$$\bar{S}_{\mathrm{T}}(\mu) = 20 \cdot \log_{10} \left(\frac{\sum\limits_{k=0}^{K-1} S_{\mathrm{T}}(\mu, k) \cdot M_{\mathrm{T}}(\mu, k)}{\sum\limits_{k=0}^{K-1} M_{\mathrm{T}}(\mu, k)} \right), \quad (2)$$

where

$$M_{\mathrm{T}}(\mu, k) = \begin{cases} 1, & \text{if } S_{\mathrm{T}}(\mu, k) > T_{\mathrm{act}} \wedge \\ & S_{\mathrm{T}}(\mu, k) = \text{ noise passage}, \\ 0, & \text{otherwise.} \end{cases} \quad (3)$$

Thus, a subband is considered for the PSD estimation when the smoothed magnitude spectrum exceeds the threshold T_{act}.

The average PSD of the processed signal is similarly defined by

$$\bar{S}_{\mathrm{P}}(\mu) = 20 \cdot \log_{10} \left(\frac{\sum\limits_{k=0}^{K-1} S_{\mathrm{P}}(\mu, k) \cdot M_{\mathrm{P}}(\mu, k)}{\sum\limits_{k=0}^{K-1} M_{\mathrm{P}}(\mu, k)} \right), \quad (4)$$

with

$$M_{\mathrm{P}}(\mu, k) = \begin{cases} 1, & \text{if } S_{\mathrm{P}}(\mu, k) > \bar{N}(\mu) \wedge \\ & S_{\mathrm{P}}(\mu, k) = \text{ noise passage}, \\ 0, & \text{otherwise.} \end{cases} \quad (5)$$

The background noise

$$\bar{N}(\mu) = 20 \cdot \log_{10} \left(\frac{1}{k_{\mathrm{end}} - k_{\mathrm{start}}} \sum_{k=k_{\mathrm{start}}}^{k_{\mathrm{end}}} |X(\mu, k)| \right) \quad (6)$$

is only estimated during the absence of any test signal between the frames k_{start} and k_{end}.

In the end, the gain alignment can be defined by $\hat{H}_{\log}(\mu) = \bar{S}_{\mathrm{T}}(\mu) - \bar{S}_{\mathrm{P}}(\mu)$ which is also smoothed in ascending and descending frequency direction by a zero-phase, first-order IIR filter. This gain alignment is bounded by a certain range

$$\hat{H}(\mu) = 10^{\left(\min\left\{ \bar{H}_{\log} + H_{\mathrm{t}},\, \max\left\{ \bar{H}_{\log} - H_{\mathrm{t}},\, \hat{H}_{\log}(\mu) \right\} \right\} / 20 \right)}, \quad (7)$$

where $\bar{H}_{\log}$ corresponds to the average logarithmic gain alignment over all frequencies and H_{t} to the boundary value.

Since the applied delay compensation depends on the sound event with the highest level, also the gain alignment is estimated by means of this sound event inside the passenger compartment.

3.3. Distance Calculation

After the estimation of the delay and the gain alignment, the actual spectral distance measure can be calculated. To this end, the same signal processing as mentioned before is applied, see Fig. 2. The resulting smoothed PSD of the test signal $S_{\mathrm{T}}(\mu, k)$ is subsequently adjusted in its gain by $S_{\mathrm{R}}(\mu, k) = S_{\mathrm{T}}(\mu, k) \cdot \hat{H}(\mu)$ and corresponds to the smoothed PSD of the reference signal. In a next step the distance between the reference and the processed PSD is calculated by

$$D(k) = \frac{\sum\limits_{\mu=\mu_S}^{\mu_E} \left| S_{\mathrm{R}}(\mu, k) - S_{\mathrm{P}}(\mu, k) \right| \cdot M_{\mathrm{tot}}(\mu, k)}{\sum\limits_{\mu=\mu_S}^{\mu_E} M_{\mathrm{tot}}(\mu, k)}, \quad (8)$$

where μ_S corresponds to the first, μ_E to the last considered sub band, and

$$M_{\mathrm{tot}}(\mu, k) = \begin{cases} 1, & \text{if } S_{\mathrm{R}}(\mu, k) > T_{\mathrm{act}} \wedge S_{\mathrm{P}}(\mu, k) > \bar{N}(\mu) \wedge \\ & S_{\mathrm{R}}(\mu, k) \wedge S_{\mathrm{P}}(\mu, k) = \text{speech passage}, \\ 0, & \text{otherwise.} \end{cases} \quad (9)$$

In a final step, the spectral distance over all active frames is calculated by:

$$\bar{D} = \frac{1}{\sum\limits_{k=0}^{K-1} M_{\mathrm{act}}(k)} \sum_{k=0}^{K-1} D(k), \quad (10)$$

where

$$M_{\mathrm{act}}(k) = \begin{cases} 1, & \text{if } \sum\limits_{\mu=\mu_S}^{\mu_E} M_{\mathrm{tot}}(\mu, k) > 0 \\ 0, & \text{otherwise.} \end{cases} \quad (11)$$

4. MODEL EVALUATION

In order to verify the reliability of the purposed measure, a subjective listening test was performed. The test is designed in style of the so-called MUlti Stimulus test with Hidden Reference and Anchor (MUSHRA) [9]. The test is a listening-only test in which the subjects compare and rate several entities in one test. Here, 16 different setups were presented to the 11 subjects, which differed in the background noise, the gender and the loudness of the speech signal, and the activation of the ICC system. The evaluation was split into two tests, where only the gender of the speech signal differed. The mean value over all subjects is taken and corresponds to $\bar{D}^{(i)}_{\mathrm{LOT}}$, where i corresponds to one of the 16 setups.

Before comparing the subjective evaluation results with the instrumental results, the results from the spectral distance measure need to be mapped to the quality scale of the subjective test. It follows that

$$\bar{D}^{(i)}_{\mathrm{map}} = a + b \cdot \bar{D}^{(i)} \,, \tag{12}$$

where i corresponds to the selected setup. The performance of the measure is derived by the correlation coefficient ρ between the results of the listening test and the measure,

$$\rho = \frac{\sum\limits_{i=0}^{I-1} \left(\bar{D}^{(i)}_{\mathrm{LOT}} - \mu_{\mathrm{LOT}}\right)\left(\bar{D}^{(i)}_{\mathrm{map}} - \mu_{\mathrm{map}}\right)}{\sqrt{\sum\limits_{i=0}^{I-1} \left(\bar{D}^{(i)}_{\mathrm{LOT}} - \mu_{\mathrm{LOT}}\right)^2 \sum\limits_{i=0}^{I-1} \left(\bar{D}^{(i)}_{\mathrm{map}} - \mu_{\mathrm{map}}\right)^2}}, \tag{13}$$

where μ_{LOT} and μ_{map} correspond to the mean value of the subjective and the instrumental evaluation results, over all setups I.

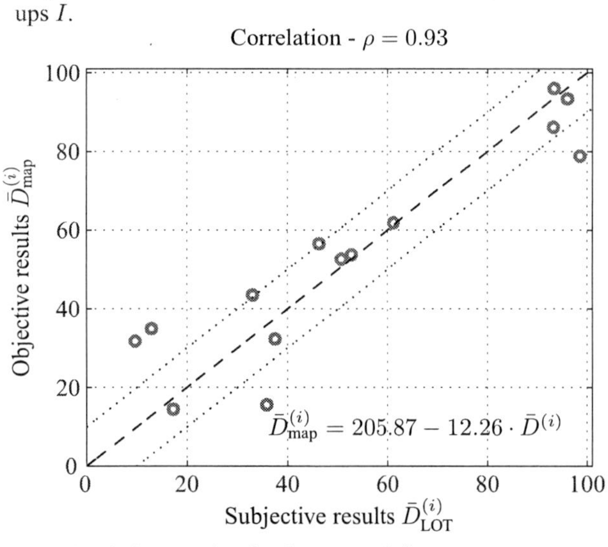

Fig. 4. Scatter plot for the spectral distance measure.

In Fig. 4, the results of the subjective and the instrumental evaluation for the 16 different setups are plotted.

5. CONCLUSION

A new measure for the evaluation of ICC systems based on a spectral distance approach was presented. The determination of the reference signal is the challenge when deriving the distance. This is reasoned in the fact that the listening passenger perceives two sound events, i.e., the direct sound and one emitted by the loudspeakers utilized by the ICC system. Therefore, a delay and gain alignment, determined by the most prominent sound event was proposed. This is reasonable since the quality of a sound event is based on the most potent, in terms of auditory perception, sound event. In order to identify the reference, the delay is estimated by a cross-correlation analysis and the changes in the spectral domain by analyzing and emitting modified noise pulses.

In addition, a subjective listening-only test was performed to verify the proposed evaluation method. The same setups were evaluated by the test subjects as well as the spectral distance. In addition, the correlation between the results of both tests was derived and a correlation of about 0.93 was achieved, see Fig. 4.

Since only a limited number of test subjects and ICC-system setups have been evaluated, further test with more subjects and other setups are required to proof the presented results. Additionally, the mapping of the instrumental results to the quality scale of the subjective evaluation could be derived in a more sophisticated way based on a larger data base.

6. REFERENCES

[1] W. V. Summers, D. B. Pisoni, R. H. Bernacki, R. I. Pedlow, and M. A. Stokes, "Effects of noise on speech production: Acoustic and perceptual analyses," *The Journal of the Acoustical Society of America*, vol. 84, no. 3, pp. 917–928, 1988.

[2] A. Ortega, E. Lleida, E. Masgrau, and F. Gallego, "Cabin car communication system to improve communications inside a car," Proc. ICASSP, Orlando, Florida, 2002.

[3] C. Lüke, H. Özer, G. Schmidt, A. Theiß, and J. Withopf, "Signal processing for in-car communication systems," 5th Biennial Workshop on DSP for In-Vehicle Systems, Kiel, Germany, 2011.

[4] K. Linhard and J. Freudenberger, "Passenger in-car communication enhancement," Proc. EUSIPCO, Vienna, Austria, 2004.

[5] U. Muesch and F. Kettler, "Instrumental testing of in-car communication systems," Proc. DAGA, Nürnberg, Germany, 2015.

[6] U. Muesch, F. Kettler, and M. Lepage, "Speech quality tests of in-car communication system," Proc. ITG Conference on Speech Communication, Braunschweig, Germany, 2012.

[7] A. Theiß, G. Schmidt, J. Withopf, and C. Lüke, "Instrumental evaluation of in-car communication systems," Proc. ITG Conference on Speech Communication, Erlangen, Germany, 2014.

[8] C. Lüke, A. Theiß, G. Schmidt, O. Niebuhr, and T. John, "Creation of a lombard speech database using an acoustic ambiance simulation with loudspeakers," 6th Biennial DSP Workshop for In-Vehicle Systems, Seoul, Korea, 2013.

[9] ITU-R Recommendation BS.1534-2, *Method for the subjective assessment if intermediate quality level of audio systems*, June 2014.

Audio-visual processing toward robust speech recognition in cars

Satoshi Tamura[1], Hiroshi Ninomiya[2], Norihide Kitaoka[2,3], Shin Osuga[4], Yurie Iribe[5], Kazuya Takeda[2], Satoru Hayamizu[1]

[1]: Gifu University, Japan
[2]: Nagoya University, Japan
[3]: The University of Tokushima, Japan
[4]: Aisin Seiki Co., Ltd., Japan
[5]: Aichi Prefectural University, Japan
E-mail: tamura@info.gifu-u.ac.jp

Abstract This paper reports our recent efforts to develop robust speech recognition in cars. Speech recognition is expected to handle many devices on cars. However, many kinds of acoustic noises, e.g. engine noise and car stereo, are observed in in-car environments, making performance of speech recognition decrease. In order to overcome the degradation, we develop a high-performance audio-visual speech recognition method. Lip images are obtained from captured face images using our face detection scheme. Some basic visual features are computed, then converted into visual features for speech recognition using a deep neural network. Audio features are obtained as well. Audio and visual features are subsequently concatenated into audio-visual features. As a recognition model, a multi-stream hidden Markov model is employed which can adjust contributions of audio and visual modalities. We evaluated our proposed method using an audio-visual corpus CENSREC-1-AV. In order to simulate driving-car condition, we prepared driving and music noises. Experimental results show that our method can significantly improving recognition performance in in-car condition.

Keywords Audio-visual speech recognition, deep neural network, multi-stream hidden Markov model, in-car speech technology.

1. INTRODUCTION

Automatic Speech Recognition (ASR) is a technique to convert human speech signals into text data. Today ASR has been widely used in many fields; for example in vehicles, ASR is employed for car navigation systems and smart cell phones as a hands-free interface. However, ASR has suffered from a crucial problem; in noisy environments recognition performance drastically decreases. In order to overcome this degradation, many works have been conducted. Audio-visual signal processing is one of the methods. Face, mouth or lip images are captured by camera and used in ASR, in addition to speech signals recorded by microphone. Basically visual data are not affected by audio noise, therefore, incorporating acoustic and visual information is much effective to improve speech recognition performance in noisy or real environments. Speech recognition employing such the visual modality is called Audio-Visual Speech Recognition (AVSR), bimodal ASR or multi-modal ASR.

This paper reports our recent efforts to develop a high-performance AVSR system applicable in vehicles. In our AVSR, we utilize a Constrained Local Model (CLM) for lip extraction. A face CLM enables us to robustly and precisely determine lip regions in face images. The model also provides lip feature points that are useful for AVSR. Furthermore, Deep Neural Network (DNN) is employed in our work. DNN is a deep-learning technique which has been widely employed in many pattern recognition and signal processing fields. There are two strategies to apply DNNs: a hybrid approach [1] and a tandem approach [2]. This paper adopts the latter method; in each modality we extract basic features, followed by computing feature vectors used in AVSR by DNN. Here we call this tandem-based feature Deep BottleNeck Feature (DBNF) [3]. A Multi-Stream Hidden Markov Model (MSHMM) is chosen in this paper. This model is conventionally used in this literature, which can control contributions of audio and visual modalities according to recognition environments.

In order to evaluate our method, we conducted recognition environments using an audio-visual corpus CENSREC-1-AV. Assuming in-car condition, we prepared training and test data sets consisting not only of noiseless data but also of in-car simulated data. We collected several noises, i.e. driving ones recorded on city roads and expressways, as well as music data as car stereo noise. These noises were overlapped to clean speech data. Recognition experiments were performed to compare our proposed system with conventional ASR schemes. We analyzed recognition results and discussion is also conducted.

The rest of this paper is organized as follows. Section 2 summarizes our AVSR system. Section 3 briefly introduces our CLM-based lip detection. Feature extraction and DBNF are described in Section 4. Recognition experiments are shown in Section 5.

2. AUDIO-VISUAL SPEECH RECOGNITION

2.1. Feature extraction

Figure 1 illustrates a feature extraction scheme in our proposed AVSR. Here we briefly introduce the feature extraction method, and details will appear in Section 4.

In the audio channel, recorded speech signals are divided into acoustic frames, at a certain frame rate and with a certain frame length. In each acoustic frame, an audio signal is converted into basic audio features: Mel-Frequency Cepstral Coefficient (**MFCC**). From an MFCC vector, an acoustic feature for recognition is obtained using an audio DNN. The acoustic feature is called Deep Bottleneck Acoustic Feature (**DBAF**).

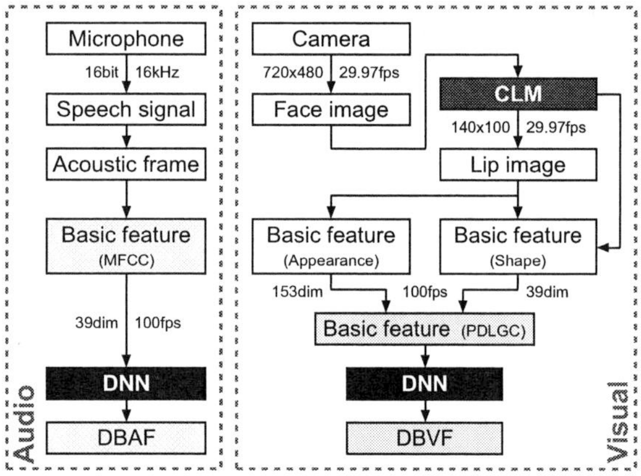

Fig. 1. Feature extraction in our AVSR.

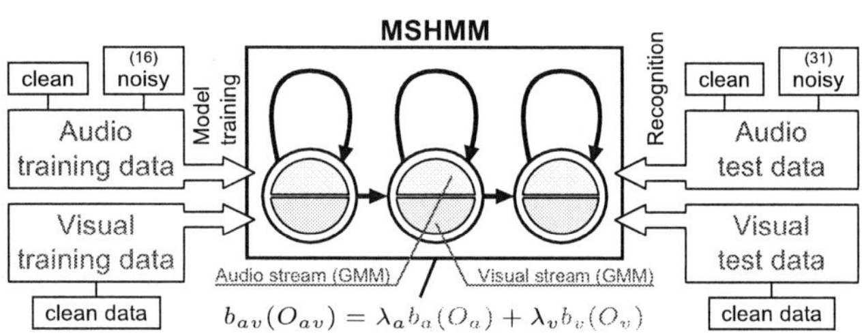

Fig. 2. A multi-stream hidden Markov Model.

In terms of the visual modality, face images are captured by camera. Subsequently, lip images are extracted from face images using a CLM. From each lip image, appearance-based and shape-based features are computed. When calculating the shape-based feature, CLM results are also utilized. By concatenating these features. an input feature vector (**PDLGC**) is obtained. Finally similar to audio features, a DNN-based visual feature vector is generated, which is called Deep Bottle Visual Feature (**DBVF**).

2.2. Modeling and decoding

An MSHMM is chosen in our system. Figure 2 depicts this model. A state in an MSHMM consists of audio and visual streams; each stream is modeled as a Gaussian Mixture Model (GMM). A log likelihood for an audio-visual vector $b_{av}(O_{av})$ is calculated as Equation (1):

$$b_{av}(O_{av}) = \lambda_a b_a(O_a) + \lambda_v b_v(O_v) \tag{1}$$

where $b_a(O_a)$ and $b_v(O_v)$ are log likelihoods for acoustic and visual features, respectively. Hyper parameters λ_a and λ_v are called stream weight factors, which control contributions of audio and visual modalities. In this paper, these factors are subject to Equation (2):

$$\lambda_a + \lambda_v = 1 \ , \ 0 \leq \lambda_a, \lambda_v \leq 1 \tag{2}$$

In our work, an audio stream is trained using not only clean speech data but also noisy speech data to enhance robustness of our recognizer against acoustic noise. A visual stream is built using clean visual features only. Decoding (recognition) is conducted applying the Viterbi algorithm, which is conventionally used in ASR.

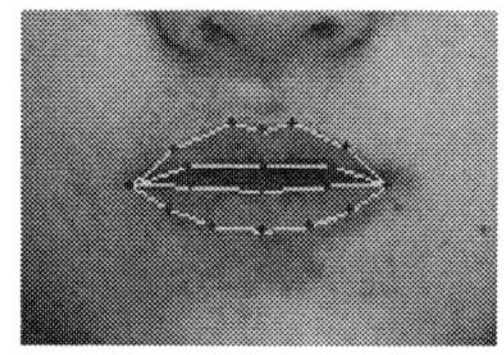

Fig. 3. An example of lip images with lip feature points.

3. LIP DETECTION

In order to compute visual features for our AVSR, extracting lip images from captured face pictures and determining lip feature points for shape-based features are needed. In face image processing, a Point Distribution Model (PDM) [4] is often used, which is a shape model of active appearance model [5]. A PDM represents face geometry parameters as a weighted linear combination of bases obtained from training data by applying Principal Component Analysis (PCA). Kojima [6] proposed a statistical face-shape model based on PDM, that enables us to conduct real-time face detection and tracking.

We adopt a CLM technique [7, 8] to robustly fit a shape model to face images. Our model is a 3D face model having eyes, nose and mouth. At first, the face model is fitted to an input frontal-face image, with estimating 3D face pose and location. Secondly, lip feature points are then estimated using a linear regression technique based on Haar-like features, while mouth model fitting is performed in which a 3D statistical mouth model is associated with the image. In this work, 18 feature points are selected as shown in Figure 3.

When clipping a lip image from a face picture, we firstly calculate a center-of-gravity point of the feature points. Let us denote an i-th lip feature point by (x_i, y_i) where $i = 1, \cdots, 18$. Now we can represent the center-of-gravity point (x_c, y_c) as:

$$x_c = \frac{1}{18}\sum_{i=1}^{18} x_i \ , \ y_c = \frac{1}{18}\sum_{i=1}^{18} y_i \tag{3}$$

A clipping window is subsequently set using the point (x_i, y_i); in this paper the window size ($W \times H$) is fixed, therefore, left-top and right-bottom points of the window must be $(x_c - W/2,\ y_c - H/2)$ and $(x_c + W/2,\ y_c + H/2)$, respectively. Figure 3 also indicates a sample lip image extracted by our method.

4. DEEP BOTTLENECK FEATURE

4.1. Basic visual feature

In this paper, four appearance-based features and one shape-based feature are employed as basic visual features. Firstly, at a t-th frame, a raster-scan vector $\boldsymbol{r}_t$ is obtained from a lip image, having intensity values of every pixels. Next, from this vector, we compute the following appearance-based features.

- **PCA**
  PCA is performed to $\boldsymbol{r}_t$ to obtain its eigenvalues. The eigenvalue vector is used as a PCA vector $\boldsymbol{f}_t^{PCA}$.
- **DCT**
  We apply 2D-DCT to $\boldsymbol{r}_t$, and coefficients are chosen in

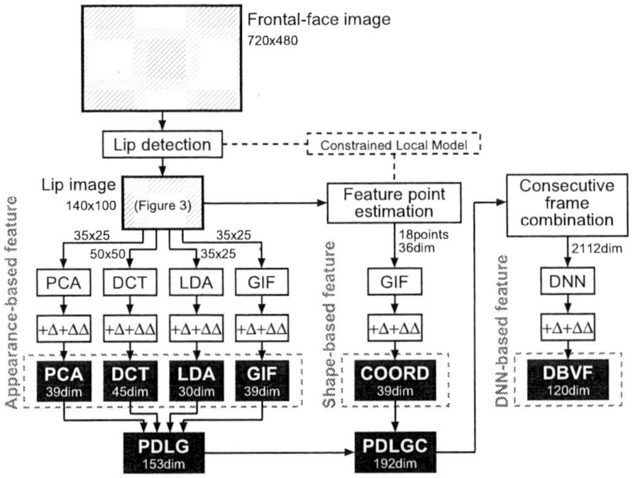

Fig. 4. Feature extraction in the visual modality.

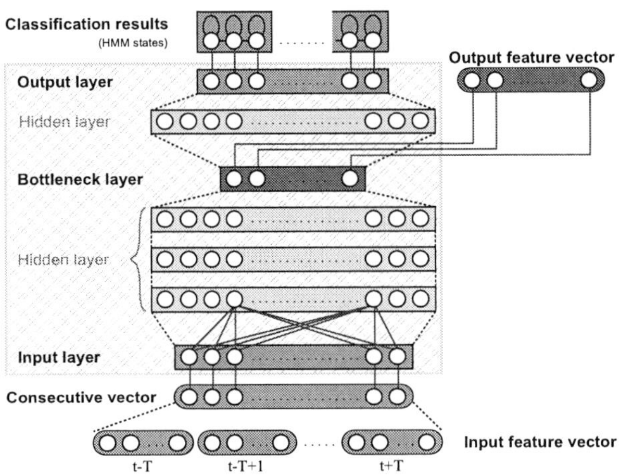

Fig. 5. A DNN for DBNF.

a zigzag manner as a DCT vector f_t^{DCT}.

- **LDA**
  LDA generates a projection matrix from r_t to f_t^{LDA}, such that variances within classes should be minimized and those between classes should be maximized.
- **GIF** [9]
  GIF consists of two projections: classification and orthogonalization / dimension reduction. In this work the former one is only applied to obtain a GIF vector f_t^{GIF}.

As a shape-based feature vector f_t^{COORD}, we use coordinates of all the 18 lip features points as:

$$c_t = \left(x_1 - x_c, y_1 - y_c, \cdots, x_{18} - x_c, y_{18} - y_c\right)^\top \quad (4)$$

Here, we additionally apply GIF to c_t so as to finally obtain f_t^{COORD}.

All the features are concatenated into a single vector. In addition, similar to an acoustic feature MFCC, time-differential coefficients are finally computed and added to the original static vector. Figure 4 shows the above process.

Table 1. Training and test data sets.

	Training set †	Test set ‡
Audio	clean, cityroad (5 SNRs), expressway (5 SNRs), music (5 SNRs)	clean, cityroad (6 SNRs), expressway (6 SNRs), music (6 SNRs), music+cityroad (6 SNRs), music+expressway (6 SNRs)
Visual	clean	clean

† 5 SNRs = 20dB, 15dB, 10dB, 5dB and 0dB
‡ 6 SNRs = 20dB, 15dB, 10dB, 5dB, 0dB and −5dB

Table 2. Feature dimensions.

Audio		Visual			
Feature	Dim	Feature	Dim	Feature	Dim
MFCC	39	PCA	39	COORD	39
DBAF	120	DCT	45	PDLG	153
		LDA	30	PDLGC	192
		GIF	39	DBVF	120

4.2. DBNF

Today DNN has been rapidly and widely employed in pattern recognition tasks. As mentioned, we use a DNN as a feature extractor. Figure 5 illustrates a DNN used in this paper, in order to compute DBNF (DBAF or DBVF) from an input basic feature. An input layer corresponds to a vector consisting not only of a current feature vector but also of previous and incoming vectors $f_{t-T}, \cdots, f_{t+T}$. In our case, an output layer is designed to match all states appeared in MSHMMs. A DNN has usually several hidden layers. In the DBNF approach, there is a bottleneck layer having relatively few units compared to the other hidden layers.

When training the DNN, concatenated input vectors and corresponding state alignment results are used. Unsupervised pre-training is conducted in a layer-wise manner [10], followed by fine-tuning all the parameters [11]. When applying the DNN, outputs obtained from all units on the bottleneck layer are composed as a DBNF vector. Audio and visual DNNs are separately built to compute DBAV and DBVF, respectively.

5. EXPERIMENT

5.1. Database

We chose a Japanese audio-visual corpus CENSREC-1-AV [12]. The task of CENSREC-1-AV is connected digit recognition. The corpus provides audio-visual training and test data sets as well as a baseline system. The training data set includes 3,234 utterances spoken by 42 subjects, while the test data set consists of 1,963 utterances made by 51 speakers. Although CENSREC-1-AV has manually clipped mouth images, in order to employ our lip extraction method and a shape-based feature, we used the original face pictures (720×480). From these pictures we automatically obtained lip images and lip feature points. The size of lip images was set as 140×100 (i.e. W=140 and H=100).

Table 3. An experimental setup of DNN.

# of units	Input	Hidden	Bottleneck	Output
DBAF	429	2,048	40	179
DBVF	2,112	2,048	40	179

	Pre-training	Fine-tuning
# of epochs	10	50
Minibatch size	256	256
Learning ratio	0.004	0.006
Momentum	0.9	0.0

Table 4. Digit recognition accuracy [%] for visual features with insertion penalty (hyper parameter) optimization.

PCA	DCT	LDA	GIF	COORD	PDLGC	DBVF
42.52	33.06	41.70	39.76	39.78	53.65	73.66

5.2. Experimental setup

When building MSHMMs and an audio DNN, we used clean speech data as well as noisy speech data. Interior driving noises recorded on cityroads and expressways, and music data as car stereo noise were prepared. Each noise was overlapped to clean speech data at the following Signal-to-Noise Ratio (SNR) levels: 20dB, 15dB, 10dB, 5dB, 0dB and −5dB. Additional noisy speech data were also made by overlapping music+cityroad and music+expressway noises, respectively. The test set includes clean and noisy data as well. Table 1 summarizes the training and test data sets.

Table 2 shows feature dimensions. The numbers of eigenvectors in PCA and LDA were set empirically. The number of classes used in LDA and GIF was 13, which corresponds to the number of visemes appeared in Japanese digit utterances [13, 14]. Experimental setup related to DNNs are shown in Table 3. We employed five hidden layers including a bottleneck layer, as Figure 5. We set T =5, meaning consecutive 11 feature vectors were incorporated as an input vector.

Model training and recognition were basically based on the baseline system in CENSREC-1-AV. Stream weight factors were manually optimized in this paper.

5.3. Result and discussion

Table 4 shows digit recognition accuracy for every visual features. At first we compared our results to the baseline accuracy using PCA provided by CENSREC-1-AV, and found they were almost the same. This means our automatic lip extraction was performed successfully. Next, compared to basic visual features, PDLGC could improve the recognition performance. And it is also found the accuracy further increased when using DBVF, indicating the effectiveness of DBNF.

Figure 6 represents recognition accuracy in ASR and AVSR. Compared to MFCC, it is obvious the performance of DBAF was better in most cases. It is also observed that our proposed AVSR scheme using DBAF and DBVF was significantly superior to the other methods. Even in low-SNR conditions, the performance was enough high with the aid of visual information. Finally Table 5 investigates AVSR performance in noise environments. The right-hand two environments consist of open-condition data. We found our AVSR achieved almost 90% accuracy in all the conditions.

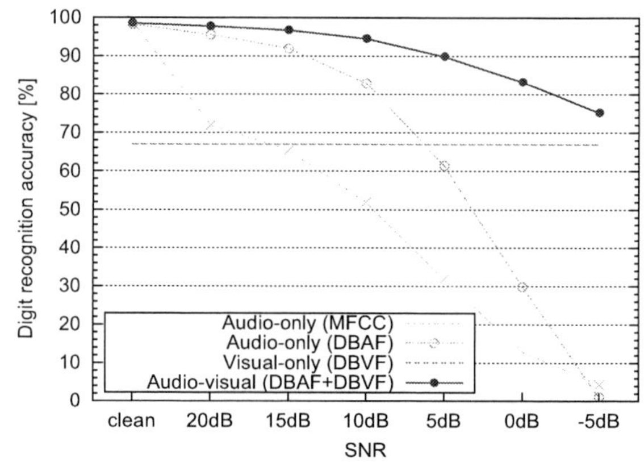

Fig. 6. Digit recognition accuracy [%] of ASR and AVSR.

Table 5. Digit recognition accuracy [%] of AVSR in several noise environments.

clean	cityroad	exp.way	music	mus+city	mus+exp
98.60	90.93	92.86	89.12	87.00	88.00

6. ACKNOWLEDGMENTS

We greatly appreciate Mr. Shinichi KOJIMA (Toyota Central R&D Labs., Inc.), for his support in lip detection and lip feature point estimation. A part of this work was supported by JSPS KAKENHI Grant Number 25730109.

7. REFERENCES

[1] A.Mohamed et al., "Acoustic modeling using deep belief networks," IEEE trans. on Audio, Speech, and Language Processing, vol.20, no.1, pp.23-29 (2012).

[2] D.Yu et al., "Improved bottleneck features using pretrained deep neural networks," Proc. INTERSPEECH2011, pp.237-240 (2011).

[3] T.Hayashi et al., "Investigation of robustness of deep bottleneck features for speakers of a variety of ages in speech recognition," Proc. Forum Acusricum 2014 (2014).

[4] T.F.Cootes et al., "Active shape models - their training and application," Computer Vision and Image Understanding, vol.61, no.1, pp.38-59 (1995).

[5] T.F.Cootes et al., "Active appearance models," IEEE trans. on Pattern Analysis and Machine Intelligence, vol.23, no.6, pp.681-685 (2001).

[6] S.Kojima, "Statistical face shape model separating inter-individual variation from intra-individual variation," IEICE technical report, vol.113, no.197, pp.13-18 (2013, in Japanese).

[7] D.Cristinacce et al., "Feature detection and tracking with constrained local models," Proc. British Machine Vision Conference, vol.3, pp.929-938 (2006).

[8] Y.Wang et al., "Enforcing convexity for improved alignment with constrained local models," Proc. CVPR2008 (2008).

[9] S.Tamura et al., "GIF-SP: GA-based informative feature for noisy speech recognition", Proc. APSIPA ASC 2012 (2012).

[10] Y.Bengio et al., "Greedy layer-wise training of deep networks," Proc. NIPS'06, pp.153-160 (2007).

[11] G.Hinton et al., "A fast learning algorithm for deep belief nets," Neural Computation, vol.18, no.7, pp.1527-1554 (2006).

[12] S.Tamura et.al., "CENSREC-1-AV: An audio-visual corpus for noisy bimodal speech recognition," Proc. AVSP2010, pp.85-88 (2010).

[13] Y.Fukuda et al., "Characteristics of the mouth shape in the production of Japanese - Stroboscopic observation", Journal of Acoustical Society of Japan, vol.3, no.2, pp.75-91 (1982).

[14] T.Seko et al., "Improvement of lipreading performance using discriminative feature and speaker adaptation," Proc. AVSP2013, pp.221-226 (2013).

Applications of the SHRP 2 Naturalistic Driving Study Data in Digital Signal Processing

Miguel Perez[1], Jonathan Hankey[2], Jonathan Antin[3], Suzie Lee[4], and Thomas Dingus[5]

[1-5]Virginia Tech Transportation Institute, Blacksburg, VA, United States
E-mail: miperez@vtti.vt.edu

Abstract Designers of Digital Signal Processing (DSP) applications in vehicles often must rely on artificial simulations and models during the development and testing phases. Existing datasets, especially naturalistic driving databases, can assist designers by allowing the development of empirically driven models and simulations. The Second Highway Research Program Naturalistic Driving Study (SHRP 2 NDS) represents the largest collection of naturalistic driving data anywhere in the world, encompassing over 3,500 different drivers and over 4,000 data years. This paper discusses the various components of the dataset and some potential uses in the area of DSP applications. More information about the SHRP 2 NDS, including access to sample data and some of the datasets mentioned herein, is also available at the SHRP 2 InSight web portal (http://insight.shrp2nds.us).

Keywords Human Factors, Naturalistic Driving, Test and Evaluation, Big Data, Safety

1 Introduction

Designers of Digital Signal Processing (DSP) applications in vehicles often must rely on artificial simulations and models during the development and testing phases. Even in situations where data acquisition in support of these activities is possible, such data collection is often time-consuming and expensive. Existing datasets, especially naturalistic driving databases, can assist designers by allowing the development of empirically driven models and simulations. For these naturalistic driving databases, volunteer drivers' behaviors are recorded via video and other sensors during the course of their normal driving routines, often for months or years.

The Second Highway Research Program Naturalistic Driving Study (SHRP 2 NDS) represents the largest collection of naturalistic driving data anywhere in the world. Encompassing over 3,500 different drivers and over 4,000 data years, it is expected to be a valuable research resource in transportation safety, operations, and logistics over several decades. The database contains over 30 million miles of driving data and spans over 2 petabytes of storage space. Dozens of research projects are currently using the database, with hundreds more expected to be initiated over the next several years.

Participants ranged from newly licensed 16 year-olds to mature drivers who were over 90 years old. Teen and older drivers were purposefully over-represented since they also tend to be over-represented in crash databases. Periods of participation generally ranged between one and two years. Data were collected continuously every time the vehicle ignition was switched on during the participation period. Data for non-consented drivers (e.g., other family members who may have used the vehicle but did not sign up to participate) was removed from the database prior to any analyses.

The data were collected between 2010 and 2013 in six different study sites across the Unites States. The sites were located in Seattle, WA, Bloomington, IN, Buffalo, NY, State College, PA, Durham, NC, and Tampa, FL. Experimental samples were larger for the Seattle, Buffalo, and Tampa sites due to their urban nature.

Vehicles in the study are slightly biased toward more recent model years because of initial experimental plan restrictions. These restrictions were eased toward the end of the study, increasing the representation of older vehicles. The primary vehicle makes sold in the United States are well represented in the vehicle sample.

Additional information about the data collection and processing can be found in [1].

The SHRP 2 NDS database includes the following datasets:

- Time series data (e.g., vehicle acceleration, location, turn rates, speed, brake pedal application, headlight status)
- Video (i.e., forward, rear, in-cabin, face)

- Driver questionnaires
- Vehicle information
- Trip summaries (offering summary information for each trip)
- Map-matching to a Roadway Information Database (providing detailed infrastructure information for trips in the database)
- Event coding (providing detailed environmental information for crashes, near-crashes, and "normal-driving" events)

The following sections will describe each of these components in additional detail, describe the process to obtain access to the SHRP 2 NDS data, and mention some potential applications of the data in the area of DSP.

2 Components of the SHRP 2 NDS

2.1 Time Series Data

The time series data are comprised of time-stamped information about the vehicle kinematics, vehicle location, and cabin environment descriptors. Measures were collected asynchronously by the data acquisition system (DAS) so that the native frequencies of the various sensors could be retained. Data collection for these measures began shortly after the ignition was switched on (there was a brief delay in the start of data collection while the DAS booted up) and lasted until the ignition was switched off.

Some of these measures were collected from the on-board vehicle network. These variables (e.g., driver seatbelt use, turn signal activation) were not available for all vehicles in the study. A partial list of the time series variables is provided below; a full list of the variables in the study is available in the data dictionaries, available on the "Background" section of the InSight website (http://insight.shrp2nds.us; more information about the website is provided in Section 3 of this paper).

- Lane Tracker (machine-vision based)
- Accelerometer Data (3 axis)
    - Included high-frequency buffer to allow for acquisition of crash pulses when a potential collision was detected
- Rate Sensors (3 axis)
- GPS
    - Latitude, Longitude, Elevation, Time, Speed, Heading
- Forward Radar
    - X and Y positions and velocities for up to eight targets
- Illuminance sensor
- Passive alcohol sensor
- Incident push button
    - Cabin audio was collected for a short interval when the button was pushed
- Vehicle network data (availability of these variables varied by vehicle)
    - Turn signals
    - Accelerator pedal position
    - Brake pedal activation
    - ABS
    - Gear position
    - Steering wheel angle
    - Speed
    - Airbag deployment

2.2 Video

There were four video views collected in a multiplexed format as part of the SHRP 2 NDS. Video was collected at a 15 Hz frequency and a resolution of 640 X 320 pixels. The views showed the forward roadway, the driver's face, the center stack and steering wheel, and the view out of the rear window (Figure 1).

The face and center stack views were illuminated with infrared light to increase the visibility of the video when light levels were low. In addition, a blurred snapshot of the cabin was collected periodically throughout each trip (Figure 2). This snapshot allows for identification of the number of passengers and, in some cases, driver and forward passenger seatbelt use.

Although the different views were merged into one video to simplify data collection, they were split during the ingestion process to increase the versatility of the dataset and safeguard participant identity.

Fig. 1. Sample video views collected during the study (from test driver).

Fig. 2. Cabin snapshot example (from test driver).

2.3 Driver Questionnaires

During the driver orientation process, shortly after agreeing to participate in the study, participants filled out a large number of questionnaires. The slate of questionnaires was designed to provide information about many aspects of participants' lifestyles, backgrounds, perceptions of driving, and medical histories. The list includes:

- Driver Demographic Questionnaire
- Driving History Questionnaire
- Driving Knowledge Survey
- Visual and Cognitive Tests
- Conner's Continuous Performance Test
- Clock Drawing Assessment
- Physical Strength Tests
- Barkley's ADHD Screening
- Risk Perception Questionnaire
- Risk Taking Questionnaire
- Sensation Seeking Scale Survey
- Driver Behavior Questionnaire
- Medical Conditions & Medications (also administered when participation ended)
- Sleep Habits Questionnaire
- Driver Exit Interview

2.4 Vehicle Information

Data acquisition system installers completed vehicle assessments as part of the instrumentation process. These assessments included the condition of the vehicle tires and battery, type of vehicle (e.g., car, SUV), powertrain, year-make-model, and whether the vehicle was equipped with certain types of infotainment features (e.g., OnStar, integrated cell phone, factory navigation, etc.).

2.5 Trip Summaries

The trip summaries contain aggregate information about the trips taken by drivers during their participation period. In total, participants in the study initiated over 5,000,000 trips. These trips account for over 130 years of continuous data. In comparison, the aggregate participation period (calendar time from the start of participation until the driver de-enrolled from the study) was over 4,000 years.

Trip summary measures include information on trip duration, distance-traveled, speed profiles, headway profiles, and types of roads traveled. Altogether, over 100 summary variables were calculated for every trip in the study. These variables are available to inform the data selection process without the need for direct access to raw study data. For example, using the trip summaries, a researcher could easily isolate trips that lasted over 30 minutes, involved traveling over 55 mph at some point during the trip, and where the maximum deceleration exceeded 0.4 g. Additional analyses would then focus only on trips that met these selection criteria.

2.6 Map-matching to a Roadway Information Database

Locating a vehicle within the driving environment is an essential element of many naturalistic driving data analyses. The map-matching process, developed at the Virginia Tech Transportation Institute (VTTI) and executed on all of the SHRP 2 NDS data, uses the sequence of GPS coordinates from the DAS to place the vehicle in pre-defined map segments. Because these map segments are known, several other analyses tasks can be simplified. For example, the identification of attributes for these segments can be semi-automated if sufficiently sophisticated GIS data are available. Likewise, finding repeat traversals over a particular segment becomes a very efficient task, often returning full result-sets in a few seconds. This map-matching process allows for the allocation of video reduction and other similar resources typically used to answer these driving context questions towards the acquisition of additional information instead.

Moreover, the map-matching process allows subsequent linking of the finalized dataset with other location-based databases. In turn, this may allow for more powerful and informed data analyses. These additional databases may include historical traffic congestion patterns, availability and characteristics of nighttime lighting, and historical weather information, among many other data elements. Work to streamline linkage to these types of databases is currently underway.

2.7 Event Coding

The coded set of events comprises over 1,500 crashes, over 2,500 near-crashes, and 20,000 “normal” driving samples (typically referred to as baselines). These events represent a simple but powerful entry point into the database. The event coding that was conducted for these instances provides detailed information on driver behavior, environmental conditions, roadway characteristics, and vehicle kinematics during each of these situations.

The crashes and near-crashes were isolated using state-of-the-art kinematic algorithms that searched for vehicle handling situations indicative of severe evasive maneuvers or vehicle impact with other objects. The baselines were sampled from the overall dataset using proportional allocation based on the amount of driving time over 5 mph for each participant, and therefore can be used to assess how often drivers are exposed to different conditions while they operate a moving vehicle.

3 SHRP 2 NDS Data Access

The SHRP 2 NDS is currently operated by VTTI and is openly available in support of research endeavors. Because this dataset was collected from volunteer participants, it constitutes Human Subjects Research and there are restrictions on its use. Therefore, access to the dataset (or portions thereof) requires approval of the proposed research by an ethics board and execution of a conditional data use license. In some cases, resources to cover data use and/or extraction costs are also required. In addition, any portions of the dataset that are identifying (e.g., face video) or potentially-identifying (e.g., GPS coordinates of the trip origin or destination) can only be accessed within a secure data enclave (currently in operation only at VTTI).

A companion site to the dataset (i.e., the InSight website; http://insight.shrp2nds.us) was created to allow researchers an initial low-barrier entry point into the database. The InSight website provides background information for the project (including data dictionaries), sample data, and copies of reports that document the data collection and processing efforts for the SHRP 2 NDS. In addition, the website provides a query functionality that allows for the merging of portions of the dataset components that have been described in this paper. Partial time series data for crashes, near-crashes, and baselines is also available, along with forward video for the crashes and near-crashes.

In addition to exploring the InSight website as a guest, which allows access to basic background information, there are two tiers of access available to interested researchers. "Registered Users" who have registered their e-mail address gain access to summary statistics for the dataset sample and to the forums page, which houses discussions about the dataset. "Qualified Researchers," who have also submitted proof of Human Subjects Research Training (available through different Institutional Review Boards and the National Institutes of Health), gain access to all of the website functionality, including the aforementioned time series and video for the crashes and near-crashes.

4 Dataset Applications to DSP

Many potential applications exist for the development and testing of DSP within in-vehicle technologies using the SHRP 2 NDS. Some examples include:

- Assessment of the frequency of occurrence for situations where in-vehicle adaptive technologies may be useful.
- Investigations of the frequency of speech interaction with in-vehicle systems and the effect of these interactions on driving behavior.
- Testing of technologies to assess driver status, including drowsiness, impairment, or distraction.
- Evaluations of existing in-vehicle interfaces to support redesign efforts.
- Testing of algorithms for driver identification and monitoring.
- Development of test situations for vehicle-to-vehicle and vehicle-to-infrastructure communications technologies.
- Development of test cases for the evaluation of semi- and fully-autonomous vehicles.

4 Conclusion

The SHRP 2 NDS is expected to serve as an invaluable research tool for decades to come. While originally envisioned as a database to support traffic safety improvements, its applications go well beyond that field. The dataset provides an unparalleled window into real-world driver behavior, which can in turn inform the design of in-vehicle systems, driver models, and vehicle instrumentation.

References

[1] Dingus, T.A., Hankey, J.M., Antin, J.F., Lee, S.E., Eichelberger, L., Stulce, K.E., McGraw, D., Perez, M., & Stowe, L. (2015). *Naturalistic Driving Study: Technical Coordination and Quality Control* (SHRP 2 Report S2-S06-RW-1). Washington, DC: Transportation Research Board.

Language ID in Vehicle

Qian Zhang[1]

University of Texas at Dallas
E-mail: qian.zhang@utdallas.edu

Abstract The abstract should be succinct with no more than 300 words [10 pt, Times New Roman]. It should be as brief as possible and concise. It should be complete, self-explanatory, and not require reference to the paper itself. The abstract should be informative giving the scope and emphasize the main conclusions, results, or significance of the work described.

Keywords Up to 5 key words characterizing the study (i.e. driver assistance, in-vehicle speech technology, human factors, active safety, traffic management, computer vision)

1 Introduction

These are instructions for authors for the 7th *Digital Signal Processing Workshop* to be held in San Francisco, CA from August, 23rd to August 25th, 2015. This document has been prepared using the required format. The electronic copy of this document can be found in:
http://ecs.utdallas.edu/dsp-2015/ (paper submissions)
The paper is to be written in two-column format.

1.1 Content of the Introduction

Background, brief literature survey and existing systems, problem definition, motivation and scope of the work are discussed here. The structure of the paper is presented (i.e. Section 2 presents formatting instructions, section 3 presents even more formatting instructions, section 5 the conclusion).

2 Formatting Instructions

MS Word Authors: Please use the MS Word template

2.1 Length

Paper length should start with a minimum of 2 pages and is limited to a maximum of 8 pages.

2.2 Section and Subsection Headings

Number section and subsection headings consecutively in Arabic numbers and type them in bold. Keep section and subsection headings always flushed left.

2.3 Tables

All tables must be numbered consecutively (in Arabic numbers). Table headings should be placed above the table. Place tables as close as possible to where they are mentioned in the main text.

Table 1. Vehicle Dynamics

Variable	**Value 1**	**Value 2**
Speed [km/h]	80	100

3 More Formatting Instructions

3.1 Figures

All illustrations should be original drawings or photographic prints of originals. Photographs should be glossy prints. Photocopies are often not good enough and should be avoided. All illustrations must be numbered consecutively (i.e., not section-wise) using Arabic numbers. Center figure captions beneath the figure (see Fig. 1). If possible, do not assemble figures at the back of your article but place them as close as possible to where they are mentioned in the main text. No part of a figure should go beyond the typing area.

DSP
in vehicles
2015

Fig. 1. DSP in Vehicle 2013 Logo.

3.2 Mathematical Formulas

Mathematical formulas should be roughly centered and have to be numbered as formula (1).

$$y=f(x) \tag{1}$$

3.3 References

References to the literature should be mentioned in the main text by an Arabic number in square brackets [1]. List these [2] (in numerical order) at the very end of your paper (under the heading References). Start each reference on a new line with its number in square brackets [3].

3.4 Fine Tuning

Make sure that abbreviations and acronyms are properly defined the first time they appear in the text. Pay attention in reviewing not only the source file (MS Word) but the PDF file as well for your draft and final versions. Make sure that pages do not end with a section or subsection heading.

5 Conclusion

We tried to keep these formatting instructions as simple as possible. A well-crafted paper is easier to read and there is more into this than only formatting. We encourage authors to pay careful attention to the quality of their English. We hope to see you in Seoul for the 6th Biennial Workshop on Digital Signal Processing in Vehicle Systems.

References

[1] A. Author1surname, B. Author2surname, "A Great Paper," in *Great Conference 1985, Optional sub-conference topic,* vol. 1234, pp. xxx-yyy, Conf. location and date, 1985.

[2] C. Author3surname, D. Author4surname, "Even a Better Paper," *THE Scientific Journal,* vol. 1, no. 1, pp. xxx-yyy, 2004.

[3] H. Kim, B. Ku, D. K. Han, S. Kang, and H. Ko, "Adaptive selection of model histograms in block-based background subtraction", *Electronics Letter*, Vol. 48, No. 8, pp. 434-435, April 2012.

Data-driven Driver Clustering based on Behavioral Primitives

Masataka Mori[1], Kazuhito Takenaka[1], Takashi Bando[2], Tadahiro Taniguchi[3], Chiyomi Miyajima[4], and Kazuya Takeda[4]

[1]: DENSO CORPORATION, Japan
[2]: DENSO International America, Inc., USA
[3]: Ritsumeikan University, Japan
[4]: Nagoya University, Japan
E-mail: masataka_a_mori@denso.co.jp

Abstract This paper presents data-driven driver clustering method based on symbolic representation. To analyze massive driving data such as corpora for naturalistic driving study efficiently, we employ non-parametric segmentation method for translating time-series driving behavior into discrete sequence of driving primitives as symbolic representation of driving. Based on frequency distribution of primitives observed during a trip, non-parametric hierarchical clustering method achieves appropriate classification of driving instructors and ordinary drivers in fully data-driven manner.

Keywords driver assistance, lane-change detection, driving behavior analysis, symbolization, hierarchical clustering

1. INTRODUCTION

Recent intelligent vehicles have various sensors for recognizing not only surrounding road environments but also operations and internal state of a driver[1]. Such driving behavioral data is gathered from driver's daily driving to analyze and predict actual potential risk for developing next generation of advanced driver assistance systems as naturalistic driving study (NDS). Since amount of the data is generally massive in NDS, direct analysis of time-series driving behavioral data becomes difficult and time-consuming.

To achieve efficient analysis of such a massive driving data, we have employed symbolization approach, which translates time-series signals into discrete symbol sequence[2]. In our approach, double articulation structure, which is well-known hierarchical structure of spoken language, is assumed to the driving behavioral data. The time-series driving data is divided into primitive segments like phonemes in spoken language, and then, they are chunked like words by using non-parametric Bayesian method.

Effectiveness of symbolization approach for representing low-level driving behaviors, e.g., breaking, turning right and so on, is already shown in several studies [3, 4]. In this paper, we focused on representing drivers' characteristics based on distribution of the symbols. Symbol frequency during a trip is modeled as word frequency in a document, and a hierarchical clustering[5] is employed for driver clustering.

Table 1. Collected driving behavioral data

	for Symbolization	for Clustering
# Drivers	433	12
Total distance	12,679 km	937 km
# Trips	5236	72
Total # Chunks	238,457	2,041
Total # Segments	416,035	5,232
Vehicle	Toyota Estimam hybrid	
Course	City roads / Expwy	Expwy
Collected data	gas & brake pedal forces, steering wheel angle, vehicle velocity etc.	

2. MATERIALS AND METHODS

We employed NUDrive corpus[6] for evaluating symbol-based driver clustering. Since we focused on drivers' characteristics, driving behavior of six instructors of driver's school and six ordinary drivers, i.e., totally 12 drivers, are extracted from NUDrive corpus for evaluation (see Table 1). All of them drove an experimental vehicle along a same course of expressway around Nagoya, Japan.

Symbol-based driver clustering consists of following four steps:

Step 1: Extract driving primitives as symbolic representation of time-series driving behavioral data

Step 2: Calculate term frequency - inverse document frequency (TF-IDF) features

Step 3: Estimate similarity of driving primitive distribution via cosine similarity

Step 4: Classify drivers' characteristics by hierarchical clustering method.

At first step, double articulation analyzer (DAA)[2] is employed for extracting driving primitives, i.e chunks in [2], in

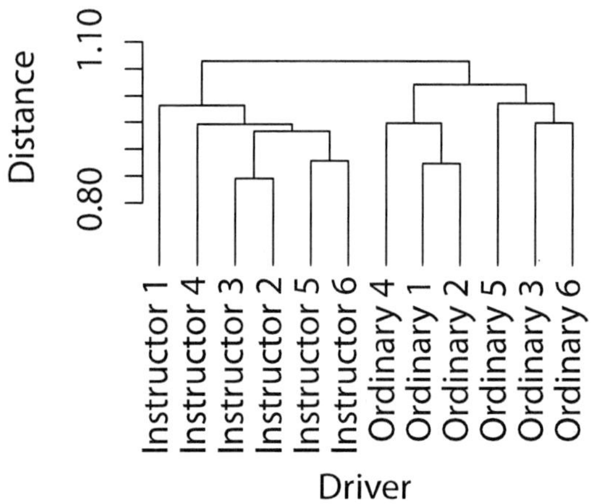

Fig. 1. Hierarchical clusters based on cosine distances between TF-IDFs of chunk bi-grams

data-driven and non-parametric Bayesian manner. Our data used for this symbolization step is shown in Table 1. For more detail of DAA, please see [2]. Second step is constructing step of feature vector. We employ TF-IDF of chunk bi-gram as feature vector, which is product of TF and IDF defined as

$$\mathrm{TF}_{k,i} = \frac{n_{k,i}}{\sum_l n_{l,i}}, \quad \mathrm{IDF}_k = \log \frac{I}{|\{d : t_k \in d\}|}, \tag{1}$$

where, $n_{k,i}$ represents frequency of chunk bi-gram k in trip i, and I is the total number of driving trip. Cosine similarity used for Step 3 is defined as the cosine of two vectors. This measure is frequently used as similarity measure between two vectors. Finally in Step 4, traditional Ward's method[5] is applied for classifying drivers' characteristics. The number of drivers' characteristics in this paper is just two, i.e., driving instructor and ordinary driver, however, we employ unsupervised clustering method because the number of driver class is generally unknown.

3. EXPERIMENTAL RESULTS

Figure 1 shows an experimental result of symbol-based driver clustering. Distance values in the figure express cosine distances between the center of gravity of clusters. As shown in this figure, instructors and ordinary drivers are separately distributed in the cosine similarity feature space with symbolic representation of driving behavior. Since the Ward's method executes clustering by minimizing sum of squared distances between drivers within class, this result shows that differences between instructors and ordinary drivers in terms of driving behavior is larger than differences within instructors or ordinary drivers. Although symbolic representation of time-series driving behavior compresses amounts of data with discarding particular information, it achieves fine driver clustering with efficient representation of drivers' characteristics according to statistical difference among driving behavior.

4. CONCLUSION

In this paper, data-driven and symbolic driver clustering method is proposed and it is evaluated using NUDrive corpus, i.e., one of the most largest driving corpora for naturalistic driving study in Japan. Data-driven symbolic representation of driving behavior achieve appropriately driver clustering, i.e., driving instructors and ordinary drivers, with efficient feature representation of time-series driving data. It is clarified from our experiment that symbolic representation keeps some kinds of characteristics information about actual driving behavior, however, drivers' characteristics consists of various point of view, e.g., gender, generation, resident area, traffic regulation, and so on. Investigating efficiency of the symbolic representation from these points is one of our important future works.

5. REFERENCES

[1] K. Bengler, K. Dietmayer, B. Farber, M. Maurer, C. Stiller, and H. Winner, "Three decades of driver assistance systems: review and future perspectives," *IEEE Intelligent Transportation Systems Magazine*, vol. 6, no. 4, pp. 6-22, 2014.

[2] T.. Taniguchi, S. Nagasaka, K. Hitomi, N. Chandrasiri, and T. Bando, "Semiotic prediction of driving behavior using unsupervised double articulation analyzer," in *IEEE Intelligent Vehicles Symposium*, pp. 849–854, 2012.

[3] A. Bender, G. Agamennoni, J.R. Ward, S. Worrall, and E.M. Nebot, "An unsupervised approach for inferring driver behavior from naturalistic driving data," *IEEE Transactions on Intelligent Transportation Systems*, 2015, *in press*.

[4] T. Bando, K. Takenaka, S. Nagasaka, and T. Taniguchi, "Unsupervised drive topic finding from driving behavioral data," in *IEEE Intelligent Vehicles Symposium*, pp. 177-182, 2013.

[5] J.H. Ward Jr., "Hierarchical grouping to optimize an objective function," *Journal of the American Statistical Association*, vol. 58, no. 301, pp. 236–244, 1963.

[6] K. Takeda, J.H. Hansen, P. Boyraz, L. Malta, C. Miyajima, and H. Abut, "International large-scale vehicle corpora for research on driver behavior on the road," *IEEE Transactions on Intelligent Transportation Systems*, vol. 12, no. 4, pp. 1609–1623, 2011.

Background Noise Effects on Automotive Hands-free Phone Call Quality and Automatic Speech Recognition

Francois Charette, John Huber, Scott Amman and Gint Puskorius

Ford Motor Company, USA
E-mail: fcharett@ford.com

Abstract: Hands-free phone calling is the most frequently utilized feature for vehicles equipped with infotainment systems and external microphones which support connection to phones and implement automatic speech recognition (ASR). However, achieving high in-vehicle hands-free phone call quality is challenging due to the extremely noisy nature of a vehicle's interior environment. Noise generated by wind, mechanical and structural sources, tire to road contact, passenger cross-talk, engine/exhaust systems, and HVAC air pressure and flow are all significant contributors to deterioration of hands-free phone call quality. In addition, other factors influencing the in-vehicle phone call quality include microphone placement, cabin acoustics, seat position of the talker, and the noise reduction algorithm of the hands-free system. In this paper, we present results of a study involving over 200 vehicles from a broad range of OEMs and vehicle segments which seeks to quantify the impact of different noise sources (particularly road and HVAC noise) on the quality of hands-free phone calling. We demonstrate that, even though the vehicles studied utilized different noise reduction / signal processing methods and demonstrated unique noise spectral characteristics for the conditions considered, some general relationships between noise level and call quality can nonetheless be observed and quantified with respect to the aggregate performance of the systems. Subsequently, we chose a single vehicle to evaluate the performance of two different suppliers' noise reduction processing capabilities. In this case, the background noise was systematically varied in level to understand the relationship between background noise level and phone call quality when the noise reduction processing and noise spectral content are controlled. The learnings generated from these studies provide a basis by which engineers can establish in-cabin vehicle noise level targets which would result in acceptable hands-free phone call quality. In addition, these processes can be used to quantify the effectiveness of a hands-free system's noise reduction processing under various noise conditions. Finally, we demonstrate that these methods can also be extended to quantifying the performance of in-vehicle automatic speech recognition. In this case, we demonstrate that word error rate (WER) is also influenced in a systematic fashion by background noise level.

Keywords Hands-free Call, Automatic Speech Recognition, NMOS, SMOS, Word Error Rate

1 Introduction

Interactions between drivers and vehicle infotainment systems are continuously increasing and have become one of the most important sources of customer dissatisfaction when the infotainment system does not operate as expected. J.D. Power Initial Quality Surveys [1] indicate that the in-vehicle infotainment system, which includes audio, communication, entertainment, and navigation sub-systems, is the most frequently cited source of things-gone-wrong for new cars, trucks, SUVs, and vans at 3 months-in-service.

The material presented in this paper is focused on the communication performance of vehicle infotainment systems. Specifically, we consider performance of the hands-free phone call and embedded automatic speech recognition systems.

1.1 Hands-free Phone Call

An infotainment system's hands-free phone system is one of the most frequently utilized features of the vehicle infotainment system. The ITU-T P1100 [2] international standard describes a battery of tests and measurements which are used to objectively quantify hands-free phone call quality. This standard covers end-to-end phone call quality, including the in-vehicle infotainment hands-free system, the driver's cellular handset and network carrier, as well as the receiver's cellular handset and network carrier. The end-to-end phone call quality is dependent on a wide range of companies that provide hardware and software services (i.e., cellular handsets and network services). It also includes all potential problems that can arise between the interfaces of hardware and services. Therefore, to keep the testing and measurements manageable and within control of what a vehicle OEM can affect, the scope of hands-free call quality results presented here are limited to the in-vehicle infotainment hands-free system. Measurements of in-vehicle infotainment hands-free system performance are obtained with a subset of the ITU-T P.1100, which is referred to as 3QUEST [3], [4] throughout this paper. The 3QUEST testing setup and metrics are summarized in section 2 of this paper.

Note that, while a vehicle's hands-free phone call system is a subset of the overall end-to-end phone call system, it is nonetheless one of the most challenging aspects to implement correctly. The performance of the hands-free phone call system is dependent on a wide range of driving conditions, resulting in a very broad range of noisy conditions which can be present in a vehicle cabin. Overall performance is also dependent on microphone design and location, the hands-free system's signal processing algorithms (filtering, noise suppression, etc.), seating position, cabin acoustic properties, and the vehicle's noise-vibration-harshness characteristics (e.g., due to wind, road, and powertrain).

1.2 Embedded Automatic Speech Recognition

Automatic speech recognition is another popular feature of a vehicle's infotainment system, which can be used to initiate phone calls (e.g., "dial #"), control music (e.g., "play artist xxx") and obtain navigation directions. In addition, ASR can be used to control certain vehicle features (e.g., "set temperature to 72 degrees"). While modern cloud-based ASR systems (e.g., Siri, Google Now) demonstrate remarkable performance, this cloud-based capability is primarily experienced in relatively quiet environments (e.g., office, home). However, this level of performance is not generally experienced in an automotive embedded ASR system, operating under a broad range of acoustic disturbances.

No established standards exist for evaluating performance of automotive embedded ASR systems. Thus, we adopt the process of recording and playing back various vehicle background noises, combined with pre-recorded close talk utterances convolved with a previously measured vehicle interior impulse response (which is unique for every interior cabin). Using this approach, varying levels of noisy utterances can be synthesized and used to test an embedded ASR system. Word error rate is then used to compare ASR performance at different background noise levels.

2 Measurement Setup

The typical laboratory measurement setup is shown in Figure 1. The right side of the diagram shows the noise simulation system used for in-laboratory reproduction of vehicle cabin noise recordings obtained on the road for the given vehicle under test. Recordings of various cabin background noise conditions were made at the hands-free microphone location. The spectral content of these background noises was reconstructed using the speaker system and equalizers as shown in Figure 1. Further details of the noise simulation can be found in [3].

2.1 3QUEST Metrics

The 3QUEST metrics from the ETSI standard [4] are presented in units of Mean Opinion Score (MOS). The 3QUEST algorithms produce three MOS metrics: (1) the Speech Mean Opinion Score (S-MOS); (2) the Noise Mean Opinion Score (N-MOS); and (3) the Global Mean Opinion Score (G-MOS). All MOS metrics are reported on a scale from 1 to 5, from lowest to highest quality, respectively. S-MOS quantifies the speech quality; it is low if the measured speech is distorted and is high if the speech sounds natural. N-MOS quantifies the noise portion of the signal; it is low if the noise is annoying and high if the noise is not perceptible. Finally, G-MOS is a metric which combines S-MOS and N-MOS into a single value. Note that these metrics are all based on extensive subjective studies, and provide a model-based prediction of a subjective evaluation. For the remainder of this paper, we will only consider the S-MOS and N-MOS metrics. We have found that G-MOS does not generally reveal any meaningful insights for automotive applications, as the signal processing algorithms are designed to trade off speech versus noise quality.

The 3QUEST algorithms require three input signals: (1) a clean speech signal that is played through to a head and torso simulator; (2) an unprocessed signal which is recorded at the hands-free microphone location; and (3) a processed signal which is collected at the Bluetooth interface between the infotainment system and the paired hands-free device (see [4] for details). The small blue boxes in Figure 1 show the points where these three signals are extracted.

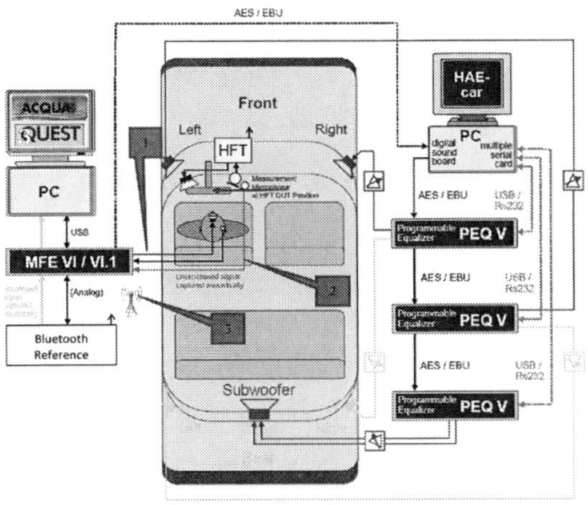

Figure 1: Laboratory setup.

3 Hands-Free Phone Call Quality Results

Performance for approximately 200 hundred vehicles, from all major OEMs and vehicle segments, was measured using the method described in section 2. Measurements were obtained for multiple background noise conditions, yielding a fairly large amount of data. We analyze all of this data to extract some general relationships of hands-free phone call quality with respect to background noise level.

As indicated above, G-MOS was not considered in this work as we have found that it is more beneficial to set targets based on the individual metrics of S-MOS and N-MOS to ensure that both the speech quality and noise reduction are adequately addressed. It has also been observed that S-MOS is less reliable as a predictor of customer response than N-MOS. Past research in our lab has shown that subjective evaluations of speech quality contain more inherent variability than those for the background noise [6]. Therefore, it would be understandable that an objective metric derived from these results would be less precise. However, S-MOS is a good first order good indicator which allows an engineer to flag potential problems, particularly if a subjective assessment is also employed.

3.1 Results Overview

Figure 2 and 3 show scatter plots of S-MOS and N-MOS results as a function of background noise level for road and HVAC fan noise, respectively. All background noise levels presented are reflective of the vehicle cabin background noise as measured at the hands-free system microphone location using an instrument grade microphone of the 3-Quest measurement system (i.e., not the microphone of the hands-free system). In addition, background noise levels were measured in what is defined in the telecommunication industry as the narrow band frequency range of 300-3400 Hz.

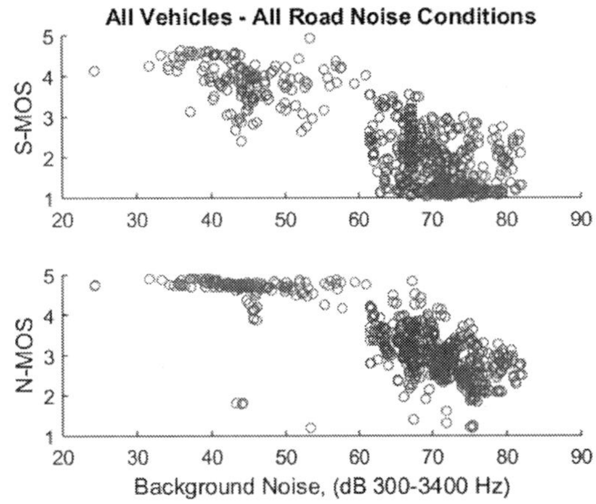

Figure 2: All road noise conditions MOS results versus narrow band background noise level.

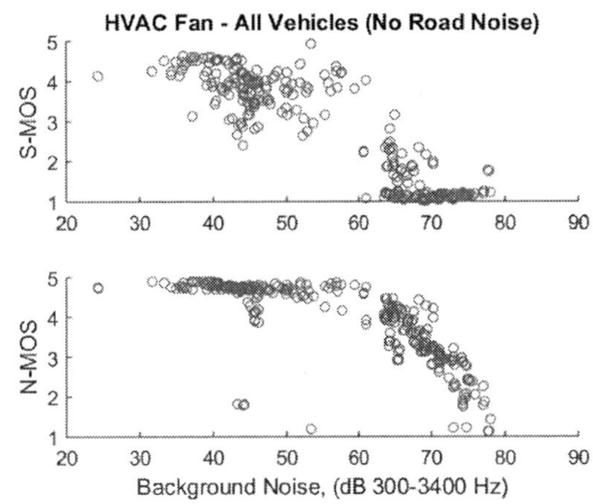

Figure 3: HVAC fan noise, all conditions, MOS results versus narrow band noise level.

3.2 Results for Road Noise

In this section, the results presented in Figure 2 are separated into the 5 road noise conditions used during testing: (1) 0 KPH (idle or no road noise); (2) 60 KPH on brushed concrete; (3) 80 KPH on brushed concrete; (4) 100 KPH on brushed concrete; and (5) 120 KPH on asphalt; these results are shown in Figures 4 through 8, respectively. In each of these scatter plots, we use a blue circle to denote individual vehicle measurements and a red dot to indicate measurement means. Histograms of MOS and background noise levels are also provided in these figures. Note that there are clear outliers in some of the scatter plots, which may possibly be due to measurements errors. These outliers were not removed simply because there are few of them and their impact on the overall results or observations presented here are not significant.

It is important to note at this point that each of the MOS score distributions (both S-MOS and N-MOS) represent what the authors call constrained populations (i.e., constrained from 1 to 5). Therefore, as the mean of a given population shifts towards a given end value, the tail of the distribution will tend to collect into that limiting value. This has the effect of producing a bi-modal looking distribution which, given enough shifting of the mean, will become a one sided uni-modal distribution.

In all of these road noise cases, where the HVAC noise was set to low and the vehicle is in motion, the scatter of N-MOS values tends to be centrally located within the range. This therefore results in a distribution of values for N-MOS that follow a uni-modal distribution. One could conclude then, that the vehicle manufacturers were successful at tuning their hands free phone call systems by attempting to remove a reasonable amount of road noise (i.e., by setting an N-MOS target at or near the central value of 3), but stopped at the point where speech would become distorted.

In the case of S-MOS, it was noted previously that the values tend to show more scatter than N-MOS. This could be partly due to the fact that S-MOS is more of a qualitative assessment metric (i.e., speech distortion), and is therefore subject to a range of opinions. Unlike N-MOS, which is derived directly from the level of background noise, S-MOS is not directly related to background noise, but is instead a measure of how much original speech was allowed to pass through the noise suppression algorithm. An additional complication is likely to occur when the background noise is sufficiently loud; here, the subjective rating may be skewed towards a lower value, even if the speech signal is mathematically undistorted from the original clean speech.

In light of these considerations, let's consider the S-MOS distributions in our study group. The scatter of S-MOS values for when the vehicle was in motion appears sufficiently large as to become bi-modal at the constraining boundary of S-MOS equal to 1. In fact, at the highest vehicle speed of 120 kph, the distribution has shifted sufficiently as to result in a one-sided uni-modal distribution at the limit of S-MOS equal to 1. This is clearly a situation where the digital signal processing had difficulty achieving a balance between reasonable noise suppression and speech distortion.

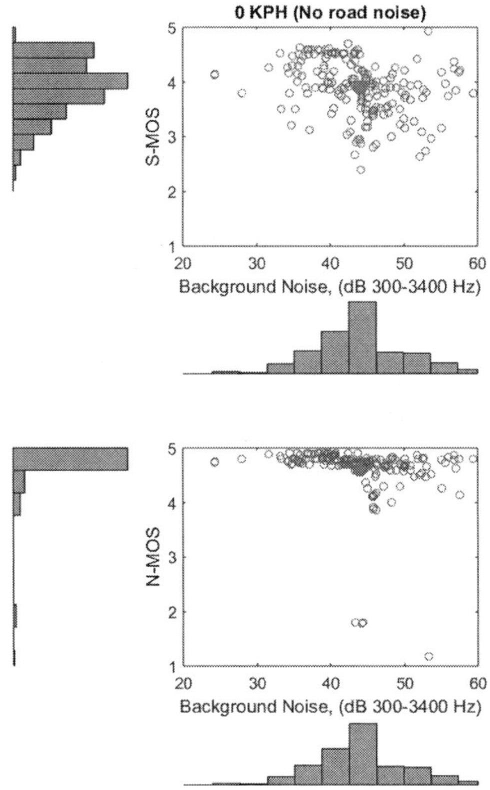

Figure 4: 0 KPH (No road noise).

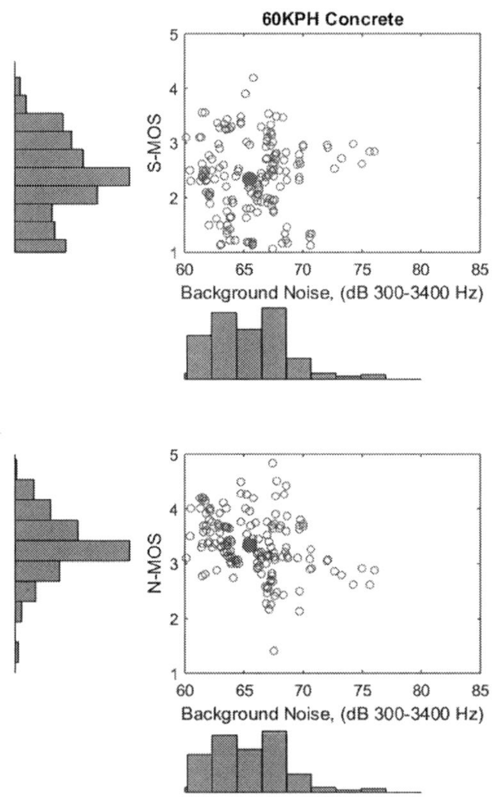

Figure 5: MOS results for 60 KPH (concrete).

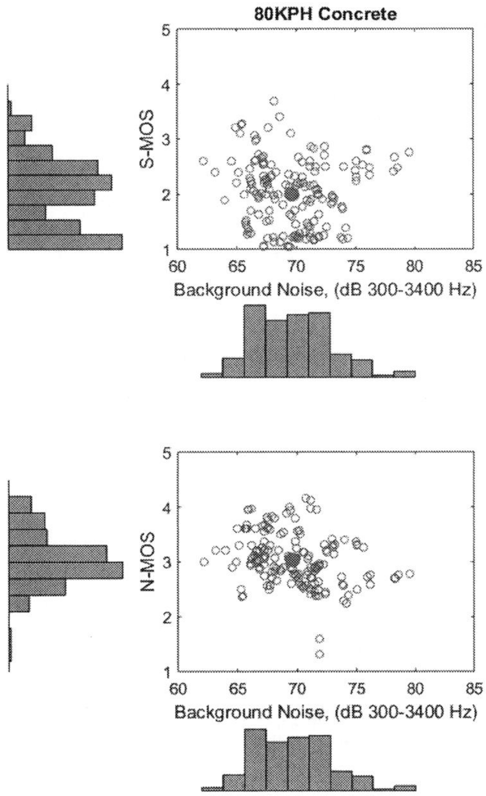

Figure 6: MOS results for 80 KPH (concrete).

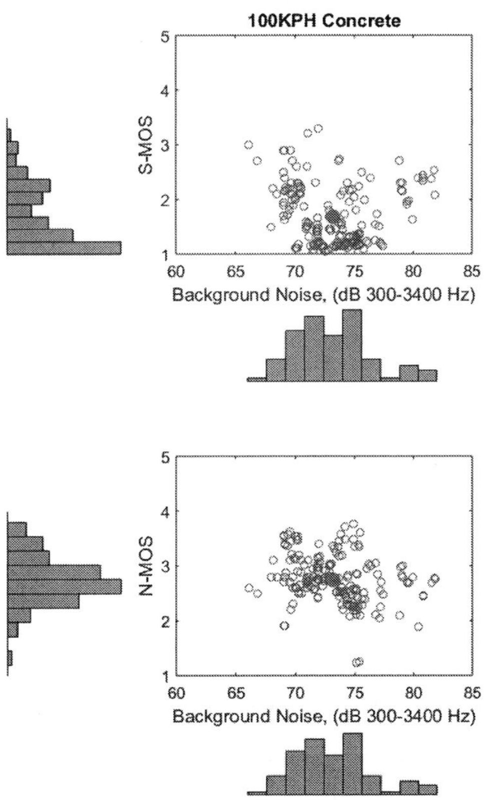

Figure 7: MOS results for 100 KPH (concrete).

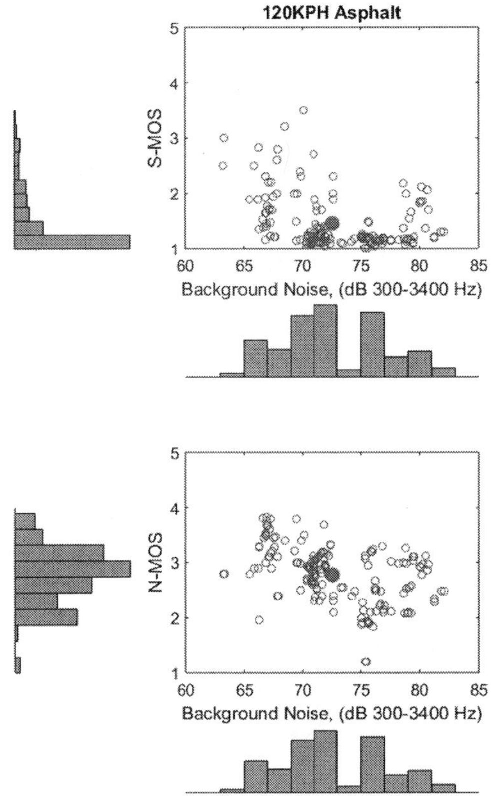

Figure 8: MOS results for 120 KPH (asphalt).

Figure 9 presents linear regression results for S-MOS and N-MOS as a function of background noise level. While the relationships between MOS scores and background noise level are expected to exhibit some nonlinearity, we use a linear correlation to extract rules of thumb to describe approximate relations between vehicle background noise level and the hands-free phone call system performance. The linear correlations are shown as black dashed lines. The S-MOS linear correlation shows a sensitivity of approximately 0.07 units of MOS lost per 1 dB of increase in background noise. Similarly, the N-MOS analysis shows a sensitivity of approximately 0.06 units of MOS lost per 1 dB of increase in background noise.

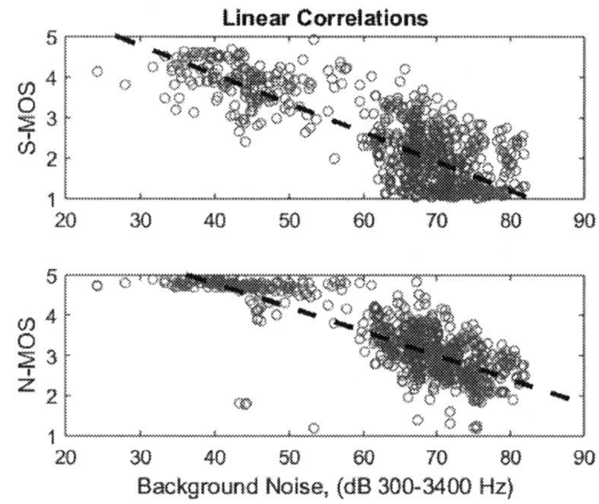

S-MOS	Linear model Poly1: f(x) = p1*x + p2 Coefficients (with 95% confidence bounds): p1 = -0.07153 (-0.07496, -0.06811) p2 = 6.925 (6.699, 7.15) Goodness of fit: SSE: 355.9 R-square: 0.6475 Adjusted R-square: 0.6471 RMSE: 0.6233
N-MOS	Linear model Poly1: f(x) = p1*x + p2 Coefficients (with 95% confidence bounds): p1 = -0.05957 (-0.0623, -0.05685) p2 = 7.171 (6.992, 7.351) Goodness of fit: SSE: 225.8 R-square: 0.6675 Adjusted R-square: 0.6672 RMSE: 0.4965

Figure 9: Correlation between MOS Results and background noise level of the grouped means.

Figure 10 shows a scatter plot of S-MOS versus N-MOS for all measurements. If N-MOS and S-MOS were thought of as being equally important and balanced, it would seem reasonable to expect that system calibrations would yield a scatter plot result with most points lying along the 45° diagonal. Given that the vast majority of the points lie to the right of the 45° diagonal, we interpret that, in general, the hands-free systems' signal processing algorithms tend to aggressively remove noise at the expense of distorting speech. This could merely be a tuning issue, or possibly a limitation of the signal processing algorithms whereby noise cannot be removed without distorting the speech above a certain noise level threshold. Since the data presented here covers a wide variety of systems, vehicles and algorithms with different tuning, we expect the latter to be the most probable explanation.

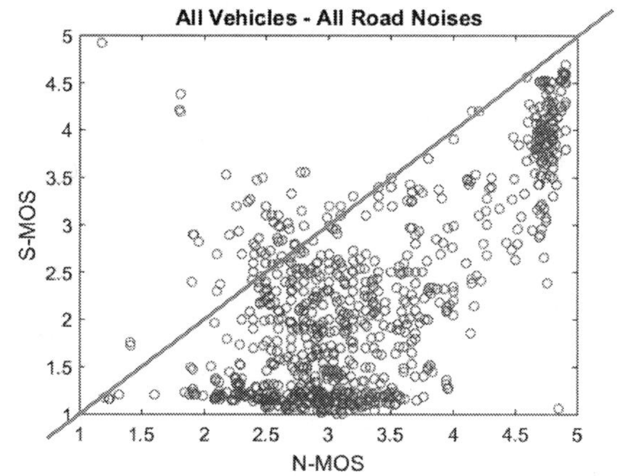

Figure 10: N-MOS versus S-MOS.

3.3 Results for HVAC

Figure 11 shows measurements for low and high HVAC fan settings in defrost mode, where green and red points denote fan low and high settings, respectively. The overall distribution of N-MOS values is somewhat similar to what was observed for the road noise results. On the other hand, the distribution of S-MOS values indicates two fan-dependent states: (1) when the HVAC fan is low, speech quality is high and essentially unaffected by the fan noise or air flow; and (2) when the HVAC fan is high, the speech quality is degraded due to fan noise and/or air flow.

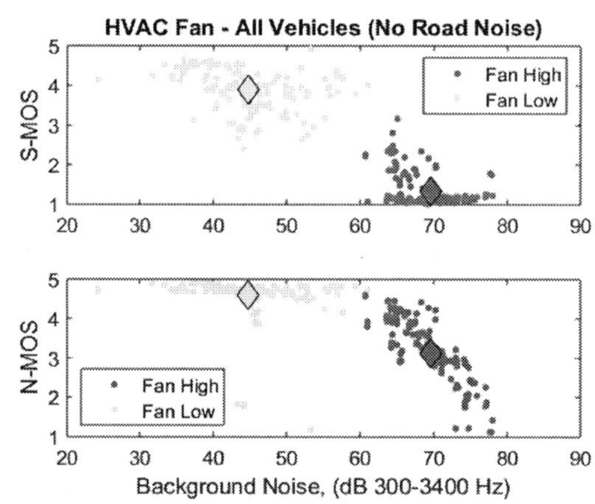

Figure 11: S-MOS and N-MOS – Grouped per HVAC fan speed.

3.4 MOS Value Variations

A multitude of noise reduction strategies exist from various suppliers of hands-free phone systems. Selecting a specific system for production should certainly be a function of how the systems perform when exposed to varying degrees of noise level.

Figure 12 shows results of an experiment in which the recorded background noise of a vehicle was reproduced inside the vehicle as described in [3]. The noise was recorded at the hands-free microphone location while driving the vehicle over a brushed concrete road surface at 100 KPH. The 0 dB setting on the graph corresponds to the actual road noise level recorded in the vehicle. The background noise level was subsequently attenuated and amplified to map out the performance of two hands-free phone systems. Again, all dB levels were calculated over the narrowband speech range of 300-3400Hz commonly used in today's hands-free phone systems.

We measured the MOS performance of two different suppliers' hands-free phone call systems at different background noise levels (attenuated and amplified). We readily observe some salient characteristics for N-MOS values in these results. Both suppliers' systems are equally affected by increases in noise level, showing an approximately 0.10 decrease in N-MOS for a 1dB increase in noise level. However, supplier B's system has an absolute advantage of 0.5 to 0.6 increase in N-MOS across all noise levels.

When considering the preservation of the speech quality, the difference between the two systems is small for low noise levels (3 dB or more below nominal). Above those noise levels, supplier A's solution exhibits a 0.3 to 0.6 S-MOS absolute advantage over that of supplier B. In this region, the system for supplier A has clearly been designed to preserve speech signal at the expense of noise reduction performance. It would be up to the automotive OEM to set the appropriate targets to balance SMOS and NMOS values to achieve proper customer satisfaction and thus determine which system was preferable.

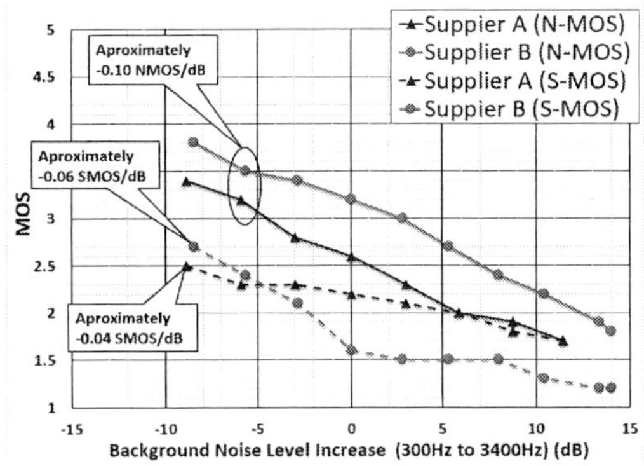

Figure 12: MOS Values versus background noise level for a given background noise.

The next example demonstrates how changing the noise suppression setting for the the hands-free phone system affects overall noise reduction (N-MOS) and speech preservation (S-MOS). Again, we evaluated two supplier systems for these purposes. We chose a background noise condition for that of a vehicle driving on an asphalt road at 120 KPH. Both suppliers' systems allowed for adjustment of noise suppression. The results are shown in Figure 13.

For both systems, N-MOS improvement with noise suppression level is approximately 0.10 N-MOS for every dB increase in noise suppression. The system of supplier A does show an advantage of at most 0.30 N-MOS at higher suppression levels. However, it can be seen that superior N-MOS performance is achieved at the expense of speech preservation, as S-MOS values decline more rapidly for the system of supplier A relative to that of supplier C. At lower noise suppression levels (0-10dB), the S-MOS values are nearly identical for both systems and are virtually unaffected by suppression level.

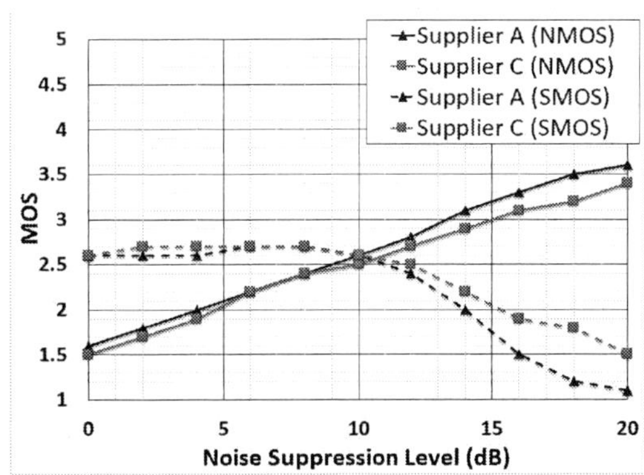

Figure 13: MOS Values versus processing noise suppression level setting.

4 Embedded Automatic Speech Recognition Results

ASR is another feature of the infotainment system which is regularly used to command a variety of functions. The ASR system uses the same vehicle acoustic path as the hands-free phone system, except that the signal is processed by the infotainment system instead of being transferred to the paired phone device.

It is possible to synthetically create a large quantity of noisy utterances and process them through an embedded ASR engine. Figure 14 shows word error rate (WER) results when the same set of utterances is mixed with five different levels of scaled vehicle background noise. Similar to the previous section, 0 dB is the nominal road noise level in the vehicle at 100 KPH on brushed concrete.

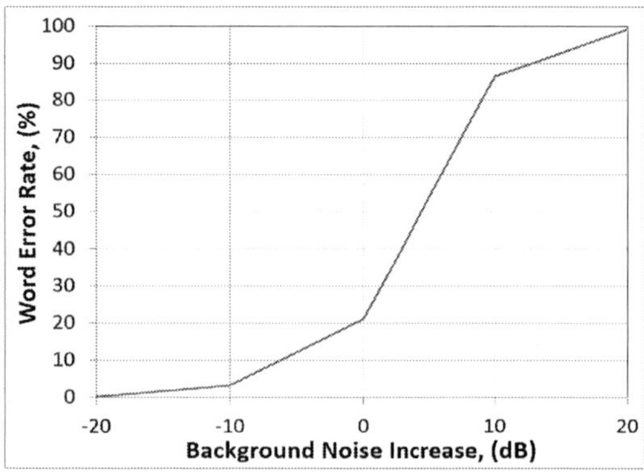

Figure 14: WER versus background noise levels.

Figure 14 shows that above the nominal (0 dB), noise level, which is highway speed, the system's performance starts to degrade dramatically

5 Conclusion

This paper has shown that existing metrics and methodologies can be applied for quantifying the quality of a hands-free phone call in an automotive environment. The examples provided in this paper show how a large population of vehicle systems behaves under various noise conditions. Two examples were also given on how MOS values can be used to both characterize noise level effects on a given system and how noise suppression level can influence phone call quality. Some of the principles developed for the quantification of hands-free phone call quality can be used as well for ASR evaluation. The simple ASR example studied demonstrates how background noise level can influence speech recognition performance. While this was only a single experiment for one particular road noise conditions, this could easily be extended to a broad variety of noise conditions. Performance could also be measured for other factors such as microphone location, seat position of the talker, cabin volume, etc.

References

[1] Youngs, J., "Modern Infotainment Systems is Top Reported Problem with New Vehicles," J.D. Power 2014 Multimedia Quality and Satisfaction Study (http://www.jdpower.com/cars/articles/car-news/modern-infotainment-systems-top-reported-problem-new-vehicles), August 28, 2014.

[2] ITU-T Recommendation P.1100, Series P: Terminals and subjective and objective assessment methods, Communications involving vehicles, Narrow-band hands-free communication.

[3] ETSI EG 202 396-1, Speech Processing, Transmission and Quality Aspects (STQ); Speech Quality performance in the presence of background noise Part 1: Background noise simulation technique and background noise database, 2008.

[4] ETSI EG 202 396-3, Speech Processing, Transmission and Quality Aspects (STQ); Speech Quality performance in the presence of background noise Part 3: Background noise transmission - Objective test methods, 2008.

[5] Head Acoustics Application Note, 3QUEST: 3-fold Quality Evaluation of Speech in Telecommunications Systems, 2008, http://www.head-acoustics.de/downloads/eng/application_notes/telecom/Appl_note_3QUEST_e0.pdf

[6] S. Amman, F. Charette, P. Nicastri, J. Huber, B. Richardson, G. Puskorius, Y. Gur, A. Cooprider, "Quantifying Hands-free Call Quality in an Automobile," Proceedings of the SAE Sound and Vibration Conference, Grand Rapids,MI,2015.

Driver Behavior Modeling on Horizontal Curves for Two-Lane Rural Roads Using In-vehicle Data Acquisition System

Sahar Ghanipoor Machiani[1], Alejandra Medina[2], Ronald Gibbons[3]

[1]: Assistant Professor, Department of Civil, Construction, and Environmental Engineering, San Diego State University, US
[2]: Senior Research Associate, Center for Infrastructure Based Safety Systems, Virginia Tech Transportation Institute, US
[3]: Director, Center for Infrastructure Based Safety Systems, Virginia Tech Transportation Institute, US
E-mail: sghanipoor@mail.sdsu.edu

Abstract

Horizontal curves on two-lane rural roads are critical segments in terms of safety since a significant number of crashes occur on them. Drivers approaching a horizontal curve perceive the curvature and make decisions on their speed and lateral position based on their perception. Understanding how drivers negotiate horizontal curves by analyzing safety surrogate measures provides practitioners with useful information for decisions on necessary countermeasures. In this study, a naturalistic driving experiment was conducted on a two-lane rural road in Virginia. Vehicles equipped by Virginia Tech Transportation Institute (VTTI) were used for the experiment. Data were collected using an installed data acquisition system (DAS) capable of collecting data on various variables such as vehicle speed, longitudinal acceleration, lateral acceleration, distance to the left lane markings, distance to the right lane markings, and vehicle path via a Global Positioning System (GPS). Collected data were analyzed for 36 participants on nine problematic curves of the corridor. Analysis of speed and lateral position was performed for specific points on the curves as well as specific sections. The results showed that drivers started decelerating 50 to 100 ft ahead of the entering point of curvature. It was also concluded that age group, gender, and radius significantly affect drivers speed on the curves. Younger males choose higher speed on the curves, but the difference between male and female drivers declines for the older group of drivers. It was found that a significant factor affecting lateral position is turn direction (right-hand/left-hand). Drivers on right-hand curves maintain a larger distance from the centerline, especially from the midpoint of curvature to the exiting point.

Keywords: human factors, traffic safety, naturalistic driving, horizontal curves, safety surrogate measures

Fig. 1: DSP in Vehicles 2015 logo

UNDERSTANDING DRIVER BEHAVIOR USING EEG BRAIN WAVES AND DEPRESSION ANXIETY STRESS SCALES (DASS-21) PSYCHOMETRIC ANALYSIS

Dini Handayani, Abdul Wahab
Kuliyyah of Information and Communication Technology, International Islamic University Malaysia
Norhaslinda Kamaruddin
Fakulti Sains Komputer dan Matematik, Universiti Teknologi Mara (UiTM), Kampus Jasin 77300 Merlimau, Jasin, Melaka, Malaysia
Hüseyin Abut
ECE Dept., SDSU, San Diego, CA (emeritus) and Boğaziçi Univ., Istanbul, Turkey
E-mail: dini.handayani@gmail.com, abdulwahab@iium.edu.my, norhaslinda@tmsk.uitm.edu.my, abut@anadolu.sdsu.edu

Abstract: Human factors account for the majority of vehicular accidents. Driving is a cognitive activity that requires total concentration, where even a small lapse can lead to fatal consequences. Some of the driver behaviors which have been shown to be factors that contribute to accidents include alcohol and drug consumption, driving in fatigued condition, and the use of cell phone. Emotional state of the people involved is another factor that affects attention and, consequently, driving behavior. Depression, anxiety, and stress are common psychiatric disorders, which can impact one's driving behavior. In this study, we proposed to analyze the driving behavior with respect to emotional state using electroencephalogram (EEG) signals and a driving simulator. These brain signals were correlated with the subjects' mood measured in terms of the Depression Anxiety Stress Scales (DASS-21). EEG results were recorded from four subjects while they performed their driving tasks on the driving simulator. The feature extraction was obtained using a Mel-frequency cepstral coefficients (MFCC) and multilayer perceptron (MLP) as the clasification technique. The results confirmed that the emotional state under the driving task is highly correlated with the DASS-21 psychometric analysis results.

Keywords: Driver behavior, negative emotion, depression, anxiety, stress.

1 Introduction

Driving is a complex cognitive task. Either consciously or unconsciously, emotional state can influence the behavior of the driver that can potentially endanger his/her life on the road.

Depression, anxiety, and stress are common psychiatric disorders that can impact one's driving behavior. Hence, it is important to measure the driver's behavior as it will help to evaluate the impact of behavioral changes on safety. Driving simulators could be employed effectively to assess driver behavior and they have been extensively used to examine the behavior in response to various physiological stimuli. Albeit limited, a good driving simulator can attempt to emulate real-life driving situations. As such, the EEG brain waves from drivers can indicate the subjects' emotional state on the road.

Here, the study of driver behavior will be investigated thoroughly in order to get concrete understanding on human emotion while driving. Thus, in this paper, the analysis of driver behavior using EEG signals and the Depression Anxiety Stress Scales (DASS-21) will be carried out. Moreover, the emotional states will be represented in terms of valence and arousal dimensions as the essential basis function.

1.2 Related Work

In an earlier study, Rizal, et. Al [1] reported that most accidents were caused by human error, possibly due to driver's behavior. The study proposed a model to classify the driver behavior using linear prediction analysis (LPA) as a feature extraction technique and Associative Neural Networks (AANN) as a classifier. The model could identify and classify the driver behavior fairly satisfactorily.

Y. Liu (2006), introduced the multitasking driving behavior model [2], where the objective was to develop a model of multitasking driver behavior based on J.R. Anderson's Adapative Control of Thought-Rational (ACT-R) cognitive architecture.

The understanding of driver behavior had been studied using a self-assessment measurement [3] and [4]. These studies utilized the Driver Behavior Questionnaire (DBQ) which hasb been videly used measurement tool to assess aspects of driver behavior. DBQ consists of three factors, namely human error, lapses, and deliberate risky actions. In a study by Matus Sucha et. al (2014) the goal was to understand the driving behavior to increase traffic safety by using DBQ [4]. Jing Shi et. al (2010), applied the DBQ to study the behavior of Chinese drivers [3]. Simililarly, Warren Harrison (2010), used the DBQ to understand the behavior of novice drivers [5].

Study with regard to the driving behavior and emotion had been done by [6] and [7]. M. van der Zwaag et. al. (2011) indicated that driving in an angry emotional state leads to antisocial driving behavior. This study also demonstated that music can intensify the effects of anger in a simulated scenario. Norzaliza et. al. (2011) reported that driver behavior has a vital connection to preventing an accident [7].

In summary, the findings from earlier studies on driving behavior has been widely reported. But none of these works have attempted to correlate the driving behavior with DASS-21 psychometric analysis. This will be the focus of our research study.

The rest of the paper is organized as follows: The emotions and mood model, experimental protocol, and the data collection procedure are discussed in Section 2. Section 3 presents and discusses the EEG signals, preprocessing, feature extraction, and the emotion classification. Section 4 presents the experimental results on DASS-21 and EEG under driving tasks. Finding are discussed in Section 5. The open issues in the current method, conclusion, and future work are discussed in Section 6.

2 Model and Analysis Methods

2.1 Emotions and Mood Model

A fairly straightforward way to represent an emotion is by using a set of categorical modalities or discrete labels, such as 'anger', 'contempt', 'disgust', 'fear', 'sad', 'surprise', and 'happy'. Psychologists frequently represent emotions and moods in an n-dimensional space. Russell [8] has proposed a two-dimensional affective space model for measuring emotions known as the circumplex model of affect. It is composed of valence and arousal. Valence ranges from negative (unpleasant) to positive (pleasant) while arousal covers from calm (low) to excited (high). As shown in Fig. 1, the corresponding dimensions (valence and arousal) are illustrated on a Cartesian coordinate space.

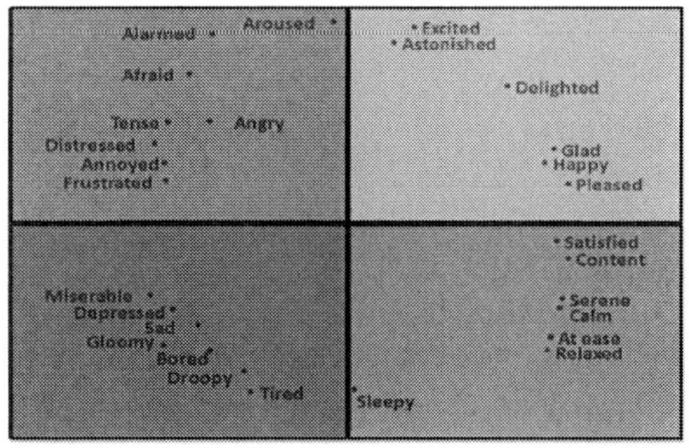

Fig. 1. Circumplex Model of Affect from [8] with the emotional state colours [9], whereby x-axis is a valence and y-axis is arousal.

Bialoskorski et. al. (2009) have depicted the emotional states with different colours [9] as illustrated in Fig. 1. Happy emotional state, indicated in orange, is defined as having a positive level of valence and a high level of arousal. Calm emotional state, indicated in green, is defined as having a positive level of valence but a low level of arousal. Sad emotional state or depression, indicated in blue, is defined as having a negative level of valence and la ow level of arousal. Fear or anxiety, indicated in red, is defined as having a negative level of valence but a high level of arousal.

2.2 Experimental Procedure and Data Collection

Four young and healthy undergraduate students (two males and two females) with different educational and cultural backgrounds have olunteered to participate in our experiments at International Islamic University of Malaysia (IIUM). Their ages varied between 20 to 29 years old, with mean (M) of 24.75 years old and standard deviation (SD) of 3.68 years. The experiments were carried out in a laboratory setting with controlled temperature and illumination. This study was formally approved by the Ethics Committee IIUM.

The subjects were briefed about the experiment and their rights through a consent form and with a verbal dialog. Subjects were explained about the interface before the experiment and during setup time. As a reference, the subjects were shown four emotions, namely "happiness", "calmness", "sadness", and "fear" by using the International Affective Picture (IAPS) concurrently with Bernard Bouchard's musical clips from [10]; one minute long for each emotion. The Depression Anxiety Stress Scale (DASS-21) [11] was used as a self-reporting mood assessment for symptoms of depression, anxiety, and stress over the past week. It is a short version of DASS-42.

The time interval for the driving task was approximately four minutes. The whole procedure took 10 minutes on average, in addition to five minutes of setup time.

3 The EEG Emotion and Mood Recognition System

3.1 EEG Signals

EEG signals were recorded using EPOC headset manufactured by Emotiv Inc. [11]. The EEG headset, as shown in Fig. 2, is used to read the driver's brain waves from the surface of the scalp. The Research Edition SDK by Emotiv Systems is a high-resolution wireless neuroheadset –14 channels plus CMS/DRL references, and P3/P4 locations-- with neuro-signal acquisition and processing functions.

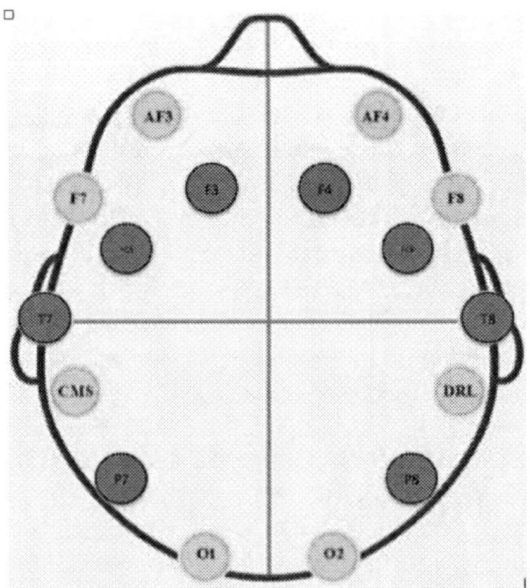

Fig. 2. The Emotiv layout for 14 EEG in addition to two reference electrodes. Layout of electrodes curtesy of Emotiv Inc. (https://emotiv.com/).

Channel label based on the International 10-20 locations are: AF3, F7, F3, FC5, T7, P7, O1, O2, P8, T8, FC6, F4, F8, and AF4. The Research Edition SDK also includes a proprietary software toolkit that contains the APIs and detection libraries. For the purpose of this study, an 8-channel EEG with a sampling rate of 128 Hz was used, as depicted in red in Fig. 2.

3.2 Preprocessing and Feature Extraction

At the preprocessing stage, EEG signals were filtered to eliminate noises and artifacts. Brain waves, which are represented by EEG signals, are commonly ranged into four bands: delta, theta, alpha, and beta. Each of the frequency bands is observed as products of different brain tasks, as some depicted in Table 1.

To extract features from the filtered signals, MFCC was adopted. Twelve linearly spaced mel filter banks were computed for each frequency band and eight EEG channels for obtaining the mel cepstrum. As a feature extraction result, 192 features were derived for each instance.

Table 1. Brainwave Signal Types

Bands	Frequency	Descriptions
Delta	0.5 Hz – 4 Hz	Deep sleep [18]
Theta	4Hz – 8 Hz	Drowsiness and fatigue due to monotonous task [19], control of working memory process [20].
Alpha	8 Hz – 13 Hz	Cognitive control [21], creative thinking [22].
Beta	13 Hz – 30 Hz	Alertness [23], phonological tasks [24].

3.3 Emotion Classification

Multilayer perceptron (MLP) was employed to construct a classifying network that output categories of emotion based on valence and arousal value inputs.

For the purpose of classification, the following network parameters were established in Table 2.

Table 2. Parameters for MLP

Parameters	Values
Number of hidden layer	1
Number of neurons in hidden layer	30
Number of neurons in output layer	1
Mean-square error goal	0.01

4 Experimental Results

4.1 DASS-21

The primary focus in this research was to assess if there was correlation between the DASS-21 psychometric analysis and the mood of subjects when performing a driving task. Table 3 shows the results of DASS-21 self-reports of drivers. Worth noting that DASS-21 self-reporting forms were filled in by the subjects just before the experiment.

DASS-21 scores consist of five levels, namely normal, mild, moderate, severe and extremely severe. Depression, anxiety, and stress symptoms typically start from moderate to extremely severe level. Thus, we consider the score levels from

Table 3. DASS-21

Subject ID	Depression	Anxiety	Stress	Gender
1	Moderate	Normal	Normal	Male
2	Moderate	Extremely Severe	Mild	Female
3	Mild	Severe	Severe	Female
4	Normal	Moderate	Mild	Male

moderate, severe, and extremely severe.

As shown in Table 3, Subject 1 is a male who has moderate level of depression, normal anxiety, and normal stress. Subject 2 is a female with moderate level of depression, extremely severe anxiety, and mild stress. Subject 3 is a female with mild depression, severe anxiety, and severe stress. Lastly, Subject 4 is a male with normal depression, moderate level of anxiety, and mild stress.

4.2 Driving Behavior Under Driving Task

Physiological signals as a primary source were used to verify the driving behavior. To get the mood in the driving task, moving average was calculated for both valence and arousal as formulated in [12]. With the smoothing average of five seconds, the result is presented in Fig. 3.

As shown in Fig. 3, the driving task visualization was based on the first minute into the experiment. The first minute is sufficient to analyze the driving behaviors of the subjects as their emotions may revert to precursor emotions after a minute into a given task which do not reflect their emotions while driving.

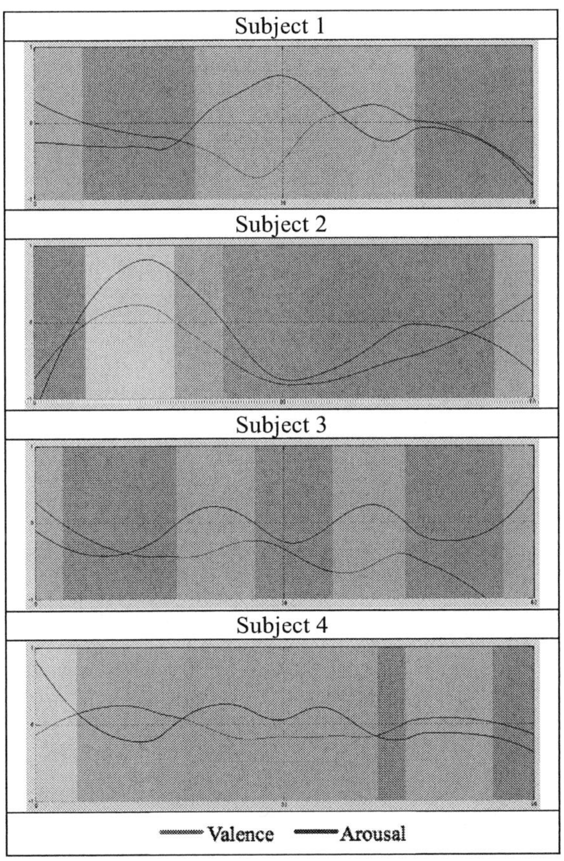

Fig. 3. Driving Task Visualization for 4 subjects

From the results and the figures we see that Subject 1 started his driving task with calm emotion, follow by sadness and fear. The mood was negative, and the dominant emotion was sadness. As shown in Fig. 3,

On the other hand, Subject 2 had various types of emotion. Her dominant mood was negative and her dominant emotion was sadness. Subject 3 was in a negative mood, with the dominant emotion being sadness. Finally, the dominant emotion for Subject 4 was fear.

5 Discussion

From the analysis results, it was observed that each subject showed diverse emotions that lead to different driver behaviors. In relation to DASS-21, depressive emotion refers to behaviors associated with feelings of sadness and worthlessness. Depression is exhibited with negative valence and low level of arousal [13]–[17].

Anxious emotion refers to behaviors associated with symptoms of physical arousal and fear. Anxiety is denoted with negative valence and high level of arousal [13]–[17].

Stressful emotion refers to behaviors associated with symptoms of general tension and irritability. Bann et. al. [13] defined stress with negative valence and high arousal [13], whereas Kanske et. al. stated that stress does not correlate with valence and arousal ratings [14].

As ilustrated in Fig. 3, the dominant emotion of Subject 1 was sadness, which correlates with depression. Referring to DASS-21, it was shown that Subject 1 was in moderate depression. Subject 1's driving behavior has reflected through the result from DASS-21.

The dominant emotion of Subject 2 was sadness, which reflects depression. Referring to DASS-21, Subject 2 was in moderate depression and extremely severe anxiety. From the driving task result, it was shown that she was depressed rather than anxious.

The dominant emotion of Subject 3 was sadness, which reflects depression. Referring to DASS-21, Subject 3 was in severe anxiety and severe stress. From the driving task result, it was shown that she was depressed rather than anxious and stressed.

Finally, the dominant emotion of Subject 4 was fear, which reflects anxiety. Referring to DASS-21, he was in moderate anxiety. From the driving task result, his driving behavior reflected the result from DASS-21.

6 Conclusions

In this study it was shown that each driver exhibited different behaviors while driving. It was also shown that the DASS-21 analysis results are correlated with drivers' behaviors. Thus, DASS-21 can be utilized for depression, anxiety, and stress analysis and it has been demonstrated through the analysis of EEG brain signals. However, it should be noted that the DASS-21 conclusions are not meant to replace a comprehensive clinical review, could be useful tool at best .

In this research study, we have attepmted to open driver behavior issues that need to be addressed in the future with more extensive testing. Performing secondary and ternary tasks while driving need to be included in the future to measure the pressure in driving and to produce different driving behaviors. An increased number of subjects can also be considered to validate the results and findings. Different feature extraction techniques and classifier methods can be considered to improve results.

References

[1] R. Othman & Z. Zhang, "Modeling Driver Operation Behavior by Linear Prediction Analysis and Auto Associative Neural Network," *Proceeding 2009 IEEE Int. Conf. Syst. Man, Cybern.*, pp. 649–653, October 2009.

[2] Y. Liu and Z. Wu, "Driver Cognitive Behavior," *3rd Int. IEEE Conf. Intell. Syst.*, no. September, 2006.

[3] J. Shi, Y. Bai, X. Ying, and P. Atchley, "Aberrant driving behaviors: a study of drivers in Beijing.," *Accid. Anal. Prev.*, vol. 42, no. 4, pp. 1031–40, Jul. 2010.

[4] M. Sucha, L. Sramkova, and R. Risser, "The Manchester Driver Behavior Questionnaire: Self-reports of Aberrant Behavior Among Czech Drivers," *Eur. Transp. Res. Rev.*, vol. 6, no. 4, pp. 493–502, Sep. 2014.

[5] W. Harrison, "Reliability of the Driver Behavior Questionnaire in a sample of novide drivers," *2009 Aus. Road Saf. Res. Polic. Educ. Conf.*, pp. 661–675, Nov. 2009.

[6] M. vander Zwaag, S. Fairclough, E. Spiridon, and J. H. D. Westerink, "The impact of music on affect during anger inducing drives," *Proc. 4th Int. Conf. Affect. Comput. Intell. Interact.*, pp. 407–416, 2011.

[7] N. Nor, A. Wahab, N. Kamaruddin, and M. Majid, "Pre-post accident analysis relates to pre-cursor emotion for driver behavior understanding," *11th WSEAS*, 2011.

[8] J. Russell, "A circumplex model of affect.," *J. Pers. Soc. Psychol.*, 1980.

[9] L. S. S. Bialoskorski, J. H. D. . Westerink, and E. L. van den Broek, "Mood Swings: An affective Interactive Art System," *ICST Inst. Comput. Sci. Soc. Informatics Telecommun. Eng. 2009*, pp. 181–186, 2009.

[10] R. Khosrowabadi, H. C. Quek, A. Wahab, and K. K. Ang, "EEG-based Emotion Recognition Using Self-Organizing Map for Boundary Detection," *20th Int. Conf. Pattern Recognition*, pp. 4242–4245, Aug. 2010.

[11] E. Epoc, "Emotiv epoc," http://emotive.com

[12] D. Handayani, H. Yaacob, A. W. A. Rahman, W. Sediono, and A. Shah, "Computational Modeling of Mood from Sequence of Emotions," *3rd Int. Conf. Internet Serv. Technol. Inf. Eng. 2015*, pp. 154–158, Feb. 2015.

[13] E.Y. Bann and J.. Bryson, "Measuring cultural relativity of emotional valence and arousal using semantic clustering and twitter," *Prepr. arXiv1304.7507*, no. 2006, 2013.

[14] P. Kanske and S. Kotz, "Auditory affective norms for German: testing the influence of depression and anxiety on valence and arousal ratings.," *PLoS One*, vol. 7, no. 1, p. e30086, Jan. 2012.

[15] L. N. Jefferies, D. Smilek, E. Eich, and J. T. Enns, "Emotional Valence and Arousal Interact in Attentional Control," *Psychol. Sci.*, vol. 19, no. 3, pp. 290–5, Mar. 2008.

[16] G. Panayiotou, R. Brown, and S. R. Vrana, "Emotional Dimensions as Determinants of self-focused Attention," *Cogn. Emot.*, vol. 21, no. 5, pp. 982–998, Aug. 2007.

[17] L. F. Barrett, "Discrete Emotions or Dimen sions ? Th e Role of Valence Focus & Arousal Focu s," vol. 12, no. 4, 1998.

[18] K. Šušmáková, "Human Sleep and Sleep EEG," Inst. of Measurement Science, Slovak Academy of Sciences," vol. 4, pp. 4–5, 2004.

[19] B.T. Jap, S. Lal, P. Fischer, and E. Bekiaris, "Using EEG spectral components to assess algorithms for detecting fatigue," *Expe. Syst. Appl.*, Vol.36, pp. 2352–2359, Mar. 2009.

[20] P. Sauseng, B. Griesmayr, R. Freunberger, and W. Klimesch, "Control mechanisms in working memory: a possible function of EEG theta oscillations.," *Neurosci. Biobehav. Rev.*, vol. 34, no. 7, pp. 1015–22, Jun. 2010.

[21] B. Zoefel, R. J. Huster, and C. S. Herrmann, "Neurofeedback training of the upper alpha frequency band in EEG improves cognitive performance.," *Neuroimage*, vol. 54, no. 2, pp. 1427–31, Jan. 2011.

[22] A. Fink, B. Graif, and A. C. Neubauer, "Brain Correlates Underlying Creative Thinking: EEG Alpha Activity in Professional vs. Novice Dancers.," *Neuroimage*, vol. 46, no. 3, pp. 854–62, Jul. 2009.

[23] J. Kamiński, A. Brzezicka, M. Gola, and A. Wróbel, "B Band Oscillations Engagement in Human Alertness Process.," *Int. J. Psychophysiol.*, vol. 85, no. 1, pp. 125–8, Jul. 2012.

[24] B. Penolazzi, C. Spironelli, C. Vio, and A. Angrilli, "Brain plasticity in developmental dyslexia after phonological treatment: a beta EEG band study.," *Behav. Brain Res.*, vol. 209, no. 1, pp. 179–82, May 2010.

Analysis of head pose as an indicator of drivers' visual attention

Sumit Jha and Carlos Busso
Multimodal Signal Processing Laboratory, Department of Electrical Engineering
The University of Texas at Dallas, Richardson TX 75080, USA
E-mail: sxj146830@utdallas.edu, busso@utdallas.edu

Abstract

Estimating the direction of visual attention is very important to predict driver's distraction, assess his/her situational awareness, and improve in-vehicle dialog systems. Tracking eye movement can be an accurate measure to identify the exact location of the gaze of the driver. However, robustly measuring gaze in a driving environment is challenging due to changes in illuminations in the vehicle, and changes in head poses from the drivers. This level of accuracy in gaze detection does not need to be perfect to understand the visual attention of the driver. Head pose provides a coarse estimate of the gaze direction, which might be helpful in determining the visual attention of the drivers for most applications. In fact, many related studies have used head pose to infer where the driver is looking. To what extent can the head pose be a useful indicator of visual attention? This paper analyzes the relation between head pose and visual attention by asking drivers to look at predefined locations in the windshield. We are interested in understanding how much the head pose deviates from the actual gaze of the driver and how much the head pose varies for a given gaze direction. We observe that the deviation is much higher in the vertical direction compared to the horizontal direction, making it more difficult to estimate vertical gaze. We observed that as the direction of attention is skewed further away from the frontal direction, the deviation between gaze direction and head pose increases. We estimate the variation in the bias as function of windshield's location, which will provide useful information about head movement of the driver to guide future in-vehicle safety system.

Keywords

In-vehicle speech technology, visual attention, active safety

AUTHOR INDEX